Map based on a survey by Clement Lempriere, first published in 1775, later republished in this hand-colored edition by Laurie & Whittle (London) in their *West-India Atlas* in 1797.

Although not as early as the several maps based on the survey of Richard Norwood conducted in the early 1600s (which produced the first detailed and accurate map of Bermuda), the "Lempriere Map" is distinctive for its appealing colors, its depiction of major relief features, and its extensive navigational notation.

(Reproduced from an antique original in the collection of Historic Urban Plans, Ithaca, New York)

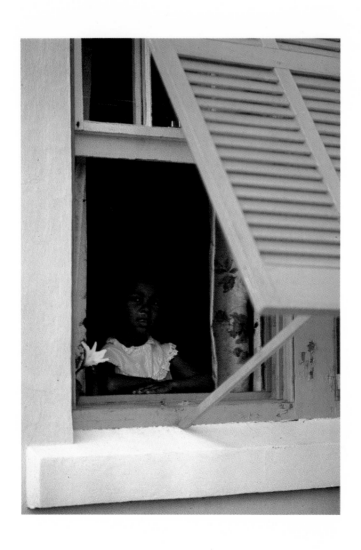

A young Bermudian in an old Bermudian setting, five-year old Tomeak Lang surveys the passing scene on one of St. George's winding lanes. The "push-out" blinds shading the window have been a fixture of the island's architecture for generations, for early settlers soon learned their value in keeping out summer sun and showers while letting in cooling breezes.

The history of this, the oldest of Britain's remaining colonies, has been a similar story writ larger: a story of a people shaping, and in turn being formed by, a tiny, special world in the midst of the vast Atlantic.

Images of Bermuda

Text and photographs by
Roger A. LaBrucherie

Imágenes Press

This book is for

Martha,
who has encouraged
me from the beginning,

and

for the people of Bermuda,
with admiration and affection
for the world they have
preserved and created

Foreword

As with my other books, in what has become a series of *Images,* this book is an attempt to capture the essence of a place and its people, primarily for those who have had only a relatively brief time to spend there.

From the time I first lived abroad, in the late 1960s, I have noticed that a newcomer's perception of a new land evolves gradually from one of great fascination (coupled with considerable ignorance), to one of near-total familiarity (coupled with becoming blasé to the differences that make every place and its people unique and potentially fascinating). Somewhere in between, I think, there is a period when understanding begins but the sense of wonder has not yet been lost. It is that perspective which I have always aspired to bring to my portrayal of a country.

Coupled with that aspiration is the belief that the modern tourist seeks to carry home more about the place he has visited than a series of post-card images. Hopefully he seeks as well some understanding of the people that make each culture unique. With Bermuda such a portrayal may be more difficult than in many places, for Bermuda is, of course, to a great extent "geared" for tourism. As Mrs. Terry Tucker, Bermuda's noted historian, has pointed out, even the island's history is sometimes popularized to make for a more salable "product."

And yet Bermuda is more, much more, than the "country as Disneyland" a friend of mine once described her as being. I had what I believe was the great good fortune of first knowing Bermuda in winter, the "off" season, when the pace slows, the island is less full of visitors, and Bermuda returns to her people. Then the sidewalks of Hamilton throng with people in tweeds and woolen scarves, and even a visitor such as myself is repeatedly greeted by passersby, in the small-town tradition which continues to make Bermuda such a delight in a world where aloofness and wariness are the rule.

Seeing Bermuda for the first time in the off season helped me see her as a complete island-nation (for, despite her formal colonial status, nearly all Bermudians think of their land as an independent country, as indeed she is in nearly all but name) with a distinct culture, and with a people who accept—indeed, insist upon—responsibility for, and who aggressively seek solutions to, their own problems. If some visitors confuse the island with a magic kingdom, all the more reason Bermudians should have a feeling of self-satisfaction with the way they have managed their domain.

Of course no book which hopes to convey a fairly complete portrait of Bermuda can ignore those aspects which make her so attractive to the tourist; but my heart is with that Bermuda of the slower pace, the occasional cold and rainy days, the small-town greeting . . .. And so it is my fervent hope that *Images of Bermuda* will convey something of that Bermuda as well to those who come to her primarily for her fabled sun, sand, and sea.

Paget Shore

Contents

Beginnings

Its 16th-Century inscription joined by scores of more recent ones, Spanish Rock* (**this page**), perched on a cliff overlooking the Atlantic near Spittal Pond, bears witness to a visitor to Bermuda—almost certainly Spanish or Portuguese—whose identity has been lost to time. The date "1543" and uncertain initials are all the record we have of his visit, but the "bones" of scores of shipwrecks lying among the reef-studded shallow waters surrounding Bermuda are ample proof that many more 16th-Century Iberians came to know Bermuda the hard way. It was a better (or luckier?) seaman, however, the Spaniard Juan Bermúdez, whom history records as the island's discoverer. He sighted, but apparently did not land on, Bermuda in the early 1500s (perhaps in 1503, and almost certainly by 1509), and to him fell the honor of the island's name. Not without some dispute, however: the English, wanting to honor Sir George Somers, the man who had been vital to the very survival of Bermuda's first English residents (see **following page**), gave the name Somers' Island to the colony. Though the Spaniard has won out in popular parlance, certain of Bermuda's formal official documents to this day carry both names.

Those scattered, and mostly unfortunate, Iberian contacts during the 1500s were the first human contacts with Bermuda which history records. Because the *conquistadores* were primarily in search of precious metals and gems, of which Bermuda was bereft, the island and its extensive reefs were seen primarily as a navigational hazard on the route home from the New World—undoubtedly a major factor in causing the Spanish to dub the island "La Isla de Demonios" (The Island of Devils, or Devil Island). Small wonder, then, that they gave Bermuda a wide berth, and that Bermuda remained uninhabited throughout the 16th Century.

Centuries of human and natural wear and tear at the rock's inscription recently led to its being capped with a bronze tablet replica, as seen in the photograph.

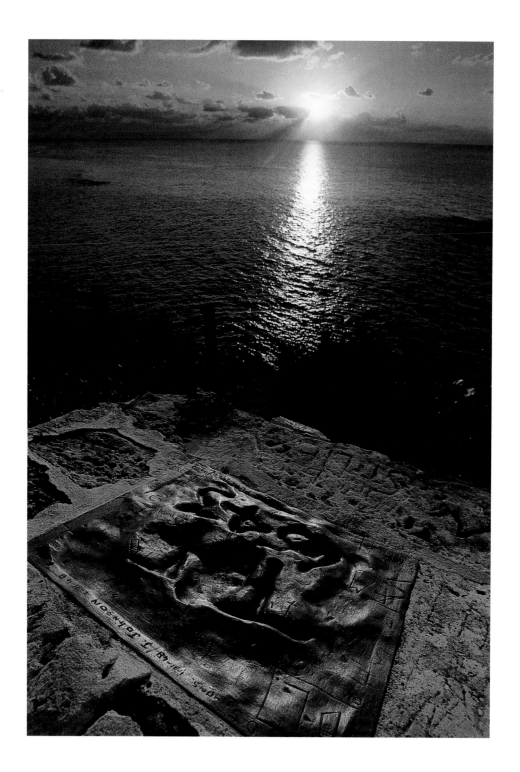

As though sailing into the storm that brought her to grief—and salvation—on the reefs of Bermuda, the *Sea Venture* rides the winds atop Hamilton's City Hall (**opposite**). The flagship of a supply fleet which set out in 1609 for Jamestown, England's fledgling colony in Virginia, the *Sea Venture* had been separated from her sister ships and buffeted for days by gale-force winds when, near sinking, land was sighted. Now the reefs, long a deadly menace to Spanish and Portuguese ships homeward bound from their New World colonies, proved kinder to the English vessel,

holding her tight in their grip until the storm subsided. The ship was a loss, but passengers and cargo made it safely to shore. The date was July 28, 1609, and Bermuda has been continuously inhabited since that day.

Under the leadership of the fleet's commander, Admiral Sir George Somers (**this page**), the castaways would spend ten months on the island, building a pair of small vessels to take them on to America.* For a place which had been known as "Devil Island," Bermuda was welcoming indeed: the climate was equable, there were no hostile natives to contend with, and there was a bountiful food supply: in addition to plentiful fish in the surrounding waters, there was an ample supply of sea turtles, the eggs and flesh of the cahow (a variety of petrel which nested on the islands), and— gift of those earlier Spanish vessels—herds of wild hogs foraging off the land. Thus the contingent from the *Sea Venture* passed nearly a year in relatively good circumstances, considering the manner of their arrival, and on May 10, 1610, the survivors— save two men left behind as deserters—set sail, reaching Jamestown two weeks later. There a shock awaited them, for they found a colony in desperate straits, having lost many of its number to starvation and Indian attacks in the previous months.

In these circumstances, Admiral Somers volunteered to return to Bermuda with a small crew to gather food for the starving Jamestown residents. This mission of mercy was to prove fatal for Sir George, however, for while on Bermuda he died of natural causes. His shipmates, after burying his heart on St. George's Island, carried his body back to England.

One of those ships, the Deliverance, is replicated on Ordnance Island, facing the town of St. George. The account of the shipwreck and the survivors' sojourn is thought to have inspired Shakespeare's play, The Tempest, which was first performed in 1611.

In the ensuing two years, the glowing account of the island related by the *Sea Venture's* survivors reached the Virginia Company of London* and persuaded it to establish a colony in Bermuda as well. Thus, in July of 1612 sixty English colonists, the first of many hundreds to be sent out by the company in the following years, landed at the island's eastern end and founded a settlement, naming it St. George, in honor both of Sir George Somers and the patron saint of England. The colonists' mission was to produce profits for the company, supposedly to be found in pearls, whale-oil, farm products (especially sugar and tobacco), and in ambergris, a substance secreted by sperm whales and highly valued in perfume-making.

The colonists enjoyed the same natural bounty and beauty which had so impressed the people of the *Sea Venture*, and the mild climate permitted year-round vegetable cultivation. (The primitive wilderness of Spittal Pond, depicted **opposite**, is today one of Bermuda's few areas suggestive of the scene those early arrivals witnessed.) It would not be long, moreover, before Bermudians would see a profit potential in the fate which had befallen the *Sea Venture*, and sometimes give fate a helping hand. Telescope to his eye, decoy bonfire lit, a "wrecker" (**this page**) searches the horizon for sign of sail—just so did some less-than-scrupulous Bermudians seek to lure unwary night-sailing sea captains in search of safe harbour onto Bermuda's uncharted reefs. (To then loot the ship of its cargo.) Though perhaps larger in legend than in actual history, the practice, together with more-common privateering (and some outright piracy), helped see Bermuda through its early lean years.

And lean years there would be, for before many years had passed the island's long-stored natural bounty of wild life would be depleted, and the colonists, many of whom had been less than keen on farming to begin with, would discover that Bermuda was ill-suited for sugar and tobacco production. Indeed, the poor showing of the colony as a commercial venture would lead to constant squabbles between the colonists and the sponsoring company, and to the eventual transfer (in 1684) of the colony's charter from the company to the Crown.** But in 1612 these developments were still far in the future; the adventurous spirits who launched the colony were undoubtedly more taken with its possibilities than with whatever drawbacks might eventually come to light.

*In 1615 the colony was passed to the related Somers Island Company.
**The term "Crown Colony" does not apply in Bermuda's case, however, for the island's settlers acquired the right of self-government during the company's tenure, and this right was never surrendered.

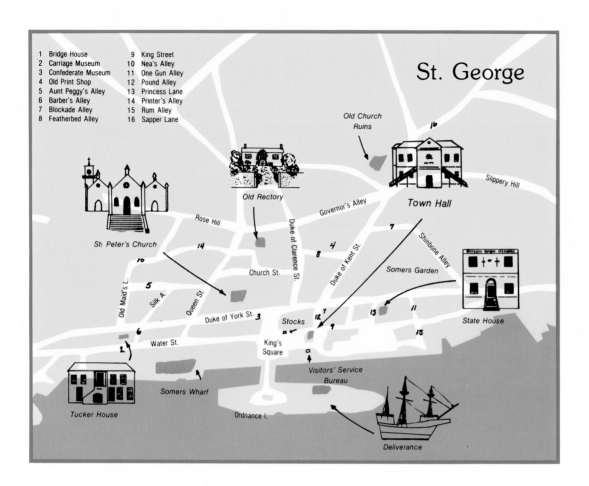

St. George

1 Bridge House
2 Carriage Museum
3 Confederate Museum
4 Old Print Shop
5 Aunt Peggy's Alley
6 Barber's Alley
7 Blockade Alley
8 Featherbed Alley
9 King Street
10 Nea's Alley
11 One Gun Alley
12 Pound Alley
13 Princess Lane
14 Printer's Alley
15 Rum Alley
16 Sapper Lane

Old Church Ruins

Old Rectory

Town Hall

Slippery Hill

St. Peter's Church

Rose Hill

Governor's Alley

Shinbone Alley

Somers Garden

Church St.

Duke of Clarence St.

Duke of Kent St.

Old Maid's L.

Silk A.

Queen St.

Duke of York St.

Stocks

King's Square

Water St.

State House

Visitors' Service Bureau

Somers Wharf

Tucker House

Ordnance I.

Deliverance

L ocated at the island's eastern extreme, on an excellent harbour and, above all, near the sole break in the encircling reefs permitting safe entry for deep-draft ships, it was natural that St. George grew to become the commercial and governmental "center" of the island. In fact, from the colony's founding, in 1612, until the establishment of Hamilton nearly 200 years later, St. George was Bermuda's only town.

Thus St. George became a concentration of some of the colony's oldest structures, such as the Old State House (the island's first stone building, built in the 1620s), the Old Globe Hotel (c. 1698), the Tucker House (c. 1711) and the Old Rectory (c. 1705, which takes its name from its one-time service as residence for the rector of the parish church of St. George's). The early pattern of narrow, twisting streets (with names like "One Gun Alley," "Old Maid's Lane," and "Featherbed Alley") leading to wharf-side King's Square, and buildings dating from the colony's first centuries characterize St. George to this day (see aerial view, **opposite**). In fact, it is probable that an 18th-Century St. Georgian, if transported to the present, would feel very much at home in St. George, so little has it changed.

J ewel of St. George, pride of the colony, St. Peter's Church (**opposite**, in a night view), has stood at the center of the island's oldest community, and at the heart of her people's affections, since the founding of St. George in 1612. (The present structure dates from 1713, although much altered and added to over the years; a complete restoration, undertaken with the view of preserving the authenticity of the building, was completed in the early 1950s).

An interior view (**this page**), looks eastward toward the red cedar altar, which, according to tradition, dates from 1612. A brass ewer glistens in a 15th-Century stone font (foreground), brought from England by the colony's earliest settlers.

St. Peter's today lays claim to being the oldest continuously-used Anglican church in the Western Hemisphere; it has, throughout its history, however, served the community for non-religious functions as well: the first meetings of Parliament were held there, as were early criminal trials. In 1970 Prince Charles there read the Throne Speech to an assemblage of dignitaries gathered to commemorate the 350th Anniversary of Bermuda's Parliament.

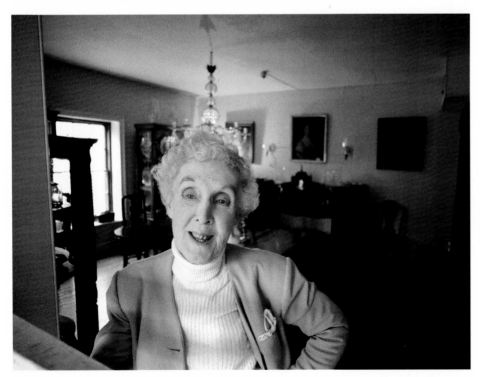

Vivid record of a shadowed past, the historic Baptismal Registry of St. Peter's Church (**upper left**), shows the matter-of-fact way in which the end of slavery in Bermuda was accepted—at least by the Anglican Church: after emancipation, which took effect on August 1, 1834, the registry simply ceases to indicate the status—"free" versus "slave"—of the child. Henceforth, *all* were free.

It goes without saying that, after two centuries of slavery, the social, economic and human adjustments to the change were far more difficult and long-lasting. It has been well argued that conditions under Bermuda's small-scale slavery may have been less arduous than those on large American and West Indian plantations; but the history of 18th-Century slave rebellions is nonetheless unmistakable evidence of the position the slaves endured.

How then, given this history, have Bermudians managed to evolve a society in which all traces of racism and rancor over past injustices are absent? The answer is quite simple: they have not. Only a Pollyanna would argue that no such traces remain. (Indeed, the colony experienced serious civil disturbance—largely racial in origin—during the late 1960s and in the 1970s.) But the following is equally clear: the vast majority of Bermudians are at ease in one another's company, white or black, and they are committed to making their island one in which those traces will steadily and completely disappear.

They are already well along that road. I think they will arrive.

* * *

Perhaps no one has contributed more to the modern widespread knowledge of Bermuda's beginnings—and to an understanding of her present—than has author-historian Terry Tucker, posed here in the museum of the Bermuda Historical Society (**lower left**). (I first met her—as has no doubt many another visiting writer in search of answers to Bermuda's puzzles—behind her desk at the Bermuda Library, clipping and filing newspaper articles for the reference section. I was as captivated by her lively personality and wit as I had been earlier by her lucid writing).

Her numerous books and articles, plus her ever-readiness to lend a hand—or a thoughtful observation—to researchers in Bermudian history, have made her, in the words of one admirer, "a national treasure of the first order."

A younger Bermudian, a resident of the island's oldest settlement, bends her head to a history lesson at the St. George's Preparatory School (**upper right**).

*　*　*

A drawing created by one of her younger schoolmates at the primary two level (**lower right**) presents a graphic explanation of Bermuda's geologic origin. Capping the extinct volcano which forms Bermuda's foundation—long ago worn away to a height below today's sea level—is a layer of aeolian limestone (composed chiefly of cemented sand and shell particles). Several hundred feet thick, this cap has been eroded over the eons to its present hilly aspect. As anyone who has seen the island from the air knows (see aerial photograph, end of chapter), the part of Bermuda showing above water covers only a small part of that volcanic submarine platform: an area perhaps ten times as large lies just below the sea's surface. Much of that submerged platform is dotted with the reefs which completely surround the island. Though often referred to as "coral reefs," they are, in fact, primarily composed of calcareous algae. (Bermuda is, thanks to the warming Gulf Stream, the most northerly point on the globe where reef-building coral is found, but coral composes only a small fraction of Bermuda's reef material.)

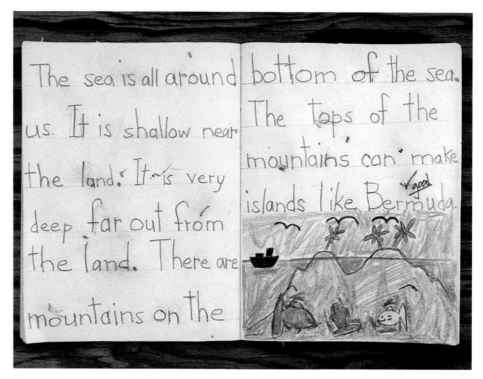

The sea is all around us. It is shallow near the land. It is very deep far out from the land. There are mountains on the bottom of the sea. The tops of the mountains can make islands like Bermuda.

Though St. George was for nearly two centuries Bermuda's only town, the rest of the colony hardly remained uninhabited, for settlers quickly spread out over the nine parishes*, which (except for St. George's) had been named for the principal shareholders of the Somers Island Company. There they established small farms and built rustic dwellings, first of wattle-and-daub, or perhaps cedar, and almost certainly roofed with thatch from the native palmetto. Later, when the threat posed by hurricanes was understood and the islanders grew more prosperous, these rude structures would be replaced by the simple houses of limestone construction which came to be known (as they are today) as the "Bermuda cottage."

Somerset, in Sandys Parish at the western end of the island, is perhaps the area where the greatest concentration of these historic farm cottages is still found—houses such as "Belfield" (**this page**), "Shrewsbury," and "Virginia Cottage"—for Somerset long remained essentially a rural area and, until the arrival of motor vehicles, remote from the changes which inevitably altered the character of the central parishes.

As each of the parishes was settled, perhaps the most important building to be constructed in each was the parish church. The Old Devonshire Church (**opposite**) on Middle Road is unique among the parish churches in remaining in the early Bermuda-cottage style. The present structure is a replica of the church built in 1716 (itself the replacement for an even earlier church on the same site built around 1623) which stood until 1970, when it was tragically destroyed by an explosion. The church became the "old" church when the parish's new stone church was constructed nearby in 1851.

*Technically speaking, the land divisions now known as parishes were originally called "tribes"; the historic name lives on in the term "tribe roads"—originally narrow lanes demarking the boundaries of the settlers' parcels of land.

It would not be until the age of air travel, of course, that a scene like the one on the **opposite page** would be witnessed, but one can well imagine that had an early Bermudian had this vantage point, he would have been shocked by the tiny dimensions of his "world." As generations of later-comers have discovered, Bermuda's rolling topography and thick vegetation deceive the eye, making it appear far larger than its scant 21 square miles.

In this view, looking toward the southwest*, St. George's Island, on the right, and St. David's Island dominate the foreground (an arm of St. David's juts into Castle Harbour at the center of the picture), while beyond, the Main Island encircles Harrington Sound and curves around the Great Sound, leading to the "tip of the fishhook," consisting of Somerset, Watford, Boaz and Ireland Islands, at upper right.

The first two centuries of the colony's history—characterized by a boom-and-bust existence dependent on subsistence farming and the various sea trades (the latter made all the more uncertain as Bermuda's long-time trading partners, the American Colonies, broke with the mother country and thus became off-limits to Bermudian vessels)—gave way to a greater degree of economic stability beginning with the 19th Century.

Though Bermudians—as Englishmen, but with close ties to the American Colonies dating from their founding—may have been divided over the issue of American independence, there could be no denying the economic benefits which came to Bermuda when her own strategic value to England was magnified by the loss of the American outposts. In 1810 the British Government began construction of the Royal Navy Dockyard on Ireland Island, a

complex vast for its time (seen **previous spread**, in an aerial view looking southward). Construction and manning of the facility would provide Bermuda with a major source of jobs and income—hence economic stability—until the mid-20th Century, when Britain's changing economic and strategic position would bring another change: the decommissioning of the yard. Thus would come to an end Bermuda's century and a half as Britain's "Gibraltar of the West." Though its strategic role is a thing of the past, the Dockyard's buildings remain as a reminder of that era. Today they house various commercial and governmental entities, as well as the Bermuda Maritime Museum, which houses an excellent collection portraying Bermuda's long involvement with the sea.

*I am indebted to the Bermuda News Bureau, and to Mr. James Babineau, photographer, for the original of this aerial view. Although I have never before used another photographer's work in my books, I was simply unable to get a shot this good—but I am grateful to Wing Commander E.M. "Mo" Ware and his little float plane for helping me try.

Heritage

Blasé to a scene repeated over and over during a busy tourist day, a St. Georgian turns a blind eye to the antics of visitors posing in the stocks in King's Square (**this page**). Though quaint today, these instruments of punishment must have put a chill in many a soul in the early days of the colony, when they were used for a more serious purpose. Together with the ducking stool and other more painful consequences (which included branding, whipping, and hanging), the punishments often seem harsh to the modern eye—especially when considered alongside their corresponding offenses. It was, it goes without saying, a different era, a time when the colony's very survival might hinge on the maintenance of a strict discipline, for the colony more than once found itself on the brink of starvation in its early years.

Happily, other, less distasteful, reminders of the island's early days have survived as well; in fact, some of them are downright tasty: "As many recipes as there are Bermudian cooks," runs the refrain when one asks the ingredients of cassava pie, Bermuda's traditional Christmas fare. As often as not the recipe is handed down from mother to daughter or granddaughter—and the traditional way requires the old bake oven adjoining the fireplace, still to be found in a few old cottages.

"There were various ways of testing the oven for the right temperature before modern stoves came along," Mrs. Barbara Henry told me. "The usual way was to put an egg shell in—if it turned brown, the temperature was hot enough—about 400 degrees. But my grandmother's cook had a very unusual way: she'd stick her head in the oven to test it!"

Mrs. Henry's ingredients, laid out on a rustic table in her early 18th-Century cottage, Stamp House (**opposite**): ground cassava root, chicken, milk, eggs, sugar, nutmeg, and salt. (Many cooks would add pork and beef as well).

Though primarily British in its roots, Bermuda's culture springs from many outside sources—Africa, the West Indies, North America, most recently—and from Bermuda herself, as the island's conditions have subtly shaped and transformed foreign traditions and created her own. Just how much foreign, how much local, influence is contained in the dance and costume of the gombeys ("gum-bays") is difficult to say. A similar custom in many of the islands of the Caribbean points irrefutably to an African origin, imported via the slave ships—while variations in costume, often mimicking local convention (such as the bobby's black helmet), reveal the indigenous contribution.

Whatever the source, the gombeys' whirling dance, to the accompaniment of drums and fife, has been on the scene—especially on traditional holidays such as New Year's, Easter Monday, and Boxing Day (December 26)—for time immemorial in Bermuda.

Opposing counsel pause during a court recess to pose for the camera (**opposite**). Their robes and wigs, descendants of 17th-Century English tradition, indicate that their case is being heard in the Supreme Court chamber (where this photograph was taken), a tribunal of both original and appellate jurisdiction in Bermuda. (Matters of a less serious nature, such as traffic violations, are heard in one of the Magistrate's Courts.) Bermuda's body of law is based on its Constitution—extensively amended and first taking written form in 1968—as well as on English Common Law.

A tradition of civility and mutual respect (perhaps aided by her small size) has kept Bermuda remarkably crime-free, although in that sense, as in many others, Bermuda—as she loses her physical and cultural isolation—is coming to resemble the outside world. (During my stay in Bermuda a referee was the target of bottles thrown during a match by irate soccer fans, an event viewed with shock by many

who had long assumed Bermuda to be exempt from such behavior. "Of course these things will happen," one elderly lady confided. "We can hardly expect to take the benefits of the modern world without getting some of the bad too. But sometimes I wonder, darlin', if we really come out ahead.")

The House of Assembly Chamber their schoolroom-for-a-day (**this page**), a class of primary-four youngsters learn the workings of Parliament from a first-hand observer, the chamber's Sergeant-at-Arms. Portraits of King George III and his Queen Charlotte adorn the wall behind the Speaker's chair; the presence of the silver Mace indicates that the "House" is in session.

The youngsters have a proud history to contemplate: the Parliament first convened in 1620, thus making it the Commonwealth's oldest representative government outside the British Isles. The system of government has undergone a steady evolution since its inception, most notably in the general extension of the franchise and the removal of its property-ownership requirement, and in the expansion of the area over which Bermudians exercise local control.

Under the 1968 Constitution the House of Assembly (composed of 40 members), and the Legislative Council (11 members) comprise the Legislature. The Governor, appointed by the British Head of State (presently Queen Elizabeth II), is responsible for external affairs, internal security and defense. The remaining Executive functions are the responsibility of the Premier (the leader of the majority party) and the Cabinet which he appoints.

The Sessions House, which houses both the Assembly Chamber and the chambers of the Supreme Court, dates from the early 1800s, when the Capital was transferred to Hamilton from St. George. The distinctive southern towers and verandah were added in 1887, to commemorate Queen Victoria's Jubilee. (See "Hamilton" for an exterior view of the Sessions House.)

The colony's Governor repeats an annual ceremony as he reviews military units drawn up for inspection on Front Street (**opposite**) in commemoration of the Queen's Birthday, celebrated officially in mid-June. Such occasions, with their traditional pomp, serve to remind Bermudians of their historic and continuing relationship with Britain, dating back nearly four centuries.

It has been a relationship which has evolved with changing conditions and ideas: as has been noted, Bermudians have had, since the earliest days of the colony, the right to enact local law (always with the proviso that they not conflict with British law, which took precedence), but the Governor, representing the Crown, historically had the most powerful voice in island affairs. As elsewhere, the trend has been to greater local self-rule, and while it would be an exaggeration to say that the Governor's role today is purely a ceremonial one, Bermuda is now essentially self-governing via its elected government.

Full independence has been, and no doubt will continue to be, debated among Bermudians. As with other colonies, Britain has indicated her willingness to accept the decision of the local majority on the matter—but it is impossible to predict which road Bermuda will choose to follow. Clearly a great many Bermudians, like this old trooper (**this page**) surveying the Queen's Birthday festivities, retain a deep pride in the island's British heritage—a pride which will weigh heavily in that choice, whatever it may be.

Braced at attention, drummer Clayton DeRosa of the Bermuda Regiment's Band awaits inspection before a Rendezvous Season performance at King's Square, St. George (**opposite**). Though usually seen by the visitor in a purely ceremonial role, the Regiment is in fact, in its principal capacity, the island's primary external defense force. (Bermuda is, of course, a part of the British Commonwealth, and as such a participant in its defense system).

The Regiment was formally constituted in 1965, growing out of two historic units—the Bermuda Rifles and the Bermuda Militia Artillery—which had seen service in both World Wars. Today all young Bermudian males register for military service, and the Regiment is made up of conscripts from that pool as well as volunteers, both male and female. In a scene more representative of their true purpose, a group of soldiers partake in training exercises at Warwick Camp, the Regiment's base, located on the south shore (**this page**).

Crossroads of Hamilton, the Perot Post Office (**opposite**, an interior view) is as much social center as it is working post office, for it seems there is seldom a moment when a couple of friends are not catching up on the latest news and gossip. Unlike St. George's, Hamilton's aspect has changed greatly since its late 18th-Century beginnings; the skyline alters inexorably under the pressure for more space from commercial, business and governmental interests. All the more reason, then that Bermudians regard the Perot Post Office with such fondness, for it represents the Hamilton of the mid-1800s, when the city had a more intimate air. (Bermudians have adopted the habits of bigger places, like using their cars and mo-peds to go across town.)

The building dates from the 1840s, when the city postmaster, William Perot, built the structure to serve as both post office and dwelling. (The adjacent park and building housing the Library, Archives and Historical Society Museum all formed part of Perot's property "Par-la-Ville.")

But Mr. Perot was to leave an even more-renowned reminder of his 40-plus years as Hamilton's postmaster: in 1848 he began combining his postal cancellation stamp, his signature, and the words "one penny" on sheets of paper—thereby creating Bermuda's first postage stamps. Of the doubtless thousands of such stamps created (Perot continued his practice until the mid-1860s, when Bermuda's first printed stamps made their appearance), only seventeen are known to still exist. In 1980 a specimen like the one pictured here (**this page, upper**), sold at auction for £70,000 (about $170,000 at 1980 exchange rates). A more familiar sight, red British-style postboxes, add splashes of color to Bermuda's landscape (**this page, lower**).

(Perot Stamp: courtesy Baron Stig Leuhusen, Hamilton).

Members of the Council of the Bermuda National Trust pose (**opposite**) before its jewel, Verdmont, an historic Smith's Parish house which has remained virtually unaltered since its construction in the early 18th Century. (Though used as a private residence until its careful restoration and conversion to a museum in the 1950s, neither plumbing nor electricity have ever been added.)

Founded in 1970, the Bermuda National Trust today brings together over 2,000 Bermudians concerned at the loss of heritage—both natural and man-made—threatened by the pace of Bermuda's recent development.

"For too long we Bermudians were oblivious to the treasures we had around us," one Trust member told me. "A lot of beautiful old houses in Hamilton, for example, were lost to some very ill-considered office buildings. We cannot—nor do we seek to—save every old structure; but there are so many pressures for 'progress' that the full price of that progress is not always considered. We already have one of the highest living standards in the world—will Bermuda be better off, if, in search of an ever-higher one and more jobs, we end up looking like Miami Beach?"

In addition to restoring, preserving, and administering architectural treasures such as Verdmont, the Old Rectory, and Springfield (in Somerset), the Trust also owns protected natural habitats such as Spittal Pond, sanctuary to a variety of migratory and resident waterfowl (**this page, upper**).

The Trust has its headquarters at the foot of Hamilton Harbour in yet another architectural gem, "Waterville" (c. 1720, **this page, lower**) a gift to the Trust from the Trimingham family.

Sea

Bermuda was born of men and women who dared the sea; among her earliest settlers were sea-faring men; and England's ascent to great-power status had depended wholly on her domination of the seas—small wonder, then, that from the earliest days of her history, Bermuda's settlers turned to the sea for their livelihoods and fortunes. Agricultural exploitation may have been high on the Somers Island Company's list of priorities, but few colonists shared that enthusiasm for the soil for very long. (Historian Terry Tucker recounts the shock of Governor William Reid at finding only two serviceable plows in the entire colony upon his arrival in 1839.)

The Bermudians' involvement in the sea (including privateering and wrecking) has been briefly noted in the first chapter. But the legitimate carrying trade was undoubtedly her greatest source of steady employment and revenue. Bermudian ships traveled the world over, earning both Bermudian sailors and shipbuilders an enviable reputation; but even the best Bermudian captains—as well as those less familiar with Bermuda's

waters—soon learned the dangers posed by the reefs encircling the island.

Thus is was natural that specialists—pilots, as they are called in maritime parlance—soon took over the task of guiding ships into St. George's Harbour; and since the hills of St. David's Island provided the best vantage point for sighting approaching ships, it was further natural that St. David's Islanders came to dominate the piloting trade. In an earlier time, before the arrival of small powered boats in the 20th Century, pilot "gigs" manned by six to eight oarsmen (such as that portrayed on a stamp issued in 1977, shown **this page**) would race to an approaching vessel; by tradition, the first to arrive got the job.

I accompanied a modern-day pilot, a veteran with more than 20 years of service, David Darrell, on a run as he guided the container ship *Oleander* on its weekly exit from Hamilton Harbour via Two Rock Passage into the Great Sound, then along the North Shore, to the passage through the barrier reef, The Narrows, off St. George's Island. "This is the only place where large vessels can get in and out," he told me as we cleared The Narrows. "Just over there's Town Cut Channel for St. George's. Now, on a small ship like this one there's not much to it—plenty of clearance all around. It's on the big cruise ships where you earn your pay."

Our conversation was interrupted as the diesel-powered launch marked "Pilots" (as seen, **opposite**, approaching a cruise ship off the mouth of St. George's Harbour) pulled alongside to take us aboard and a rope ladder was dropped over *Oleander's* side. "It's sure a lot easier getting to and from the ships than it was in the old days," he commented once we had transferred to the pilot boat. "You know, those gigs would race fifty miles sometimes to get their pilot to the ship first. That's a lot of rowing!"

That historic tradition came to an end in 1929, when the government took over the service. As with many traditions, progress—this time in the form of modern ships and their insurers—had spelled the doom of the seat-of-the-pants, catch-as-catch-can piloting days.

BERMUDA
PILOTING
17 CENTS
EIIR

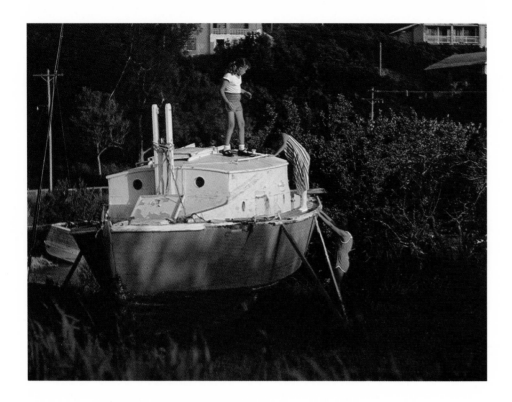

With its proud history in the piloting trade it is no wonder that to this day St. David's Island continues to supply many of the pilots and men who crew the pilot boats—men such as Skipper Headley Millett and Engineer James Foggo (right and left respectively, in the picture **opposite**), of the pilot boat *St. Brendan*, who have been together in the trade since their teens. Like nearly all their fellow islanders, they have a reputation for sturdiness and independence of spirit (perhaps due to an infusion of blood of Mahican Indians from America, who formed a part of the early slave population) which is almost legendary in Bermuda—and since they are both well into their seventies, and show no inclination to retire anytime soon, it seems a reputation well earned.

Though the linking, in the 1930s, of St. David's to the remainder of Bermuda by bridge ended forever St. David's historic physical isolation, there is no denying that St. David's continues to be a world apart. It is perhaps, as one Bermudian told me, a difference more easily felt than seen, although some differences come to the eye as well: nowhere else are so many wooden houses still standing; nowhere else does the motor vehicle—indeed, all the trappings of the 20th Century—seem so far away; nowhere else does the pace seem so measured (even the St. David's Islander's speech seems slower); but, above all, nowhere else has the sea remained so close to the center of life. (For all Hamilton's fine restaurants, a Bermudian will tell you, the finest seafood dinners are still to be found in the kitchens of St. David's Island.)

Thus a long-abandoned fishing boat (**this page**) blends naturally with the surroundings and becomes a playground for neighborhood children; and a St. David's home would be incomplete without the mariner's old stand-by, the shark-oil barometer—the likelihood of bad weather ahead increasing as the cloudiness at the bottom of the bottle rises.

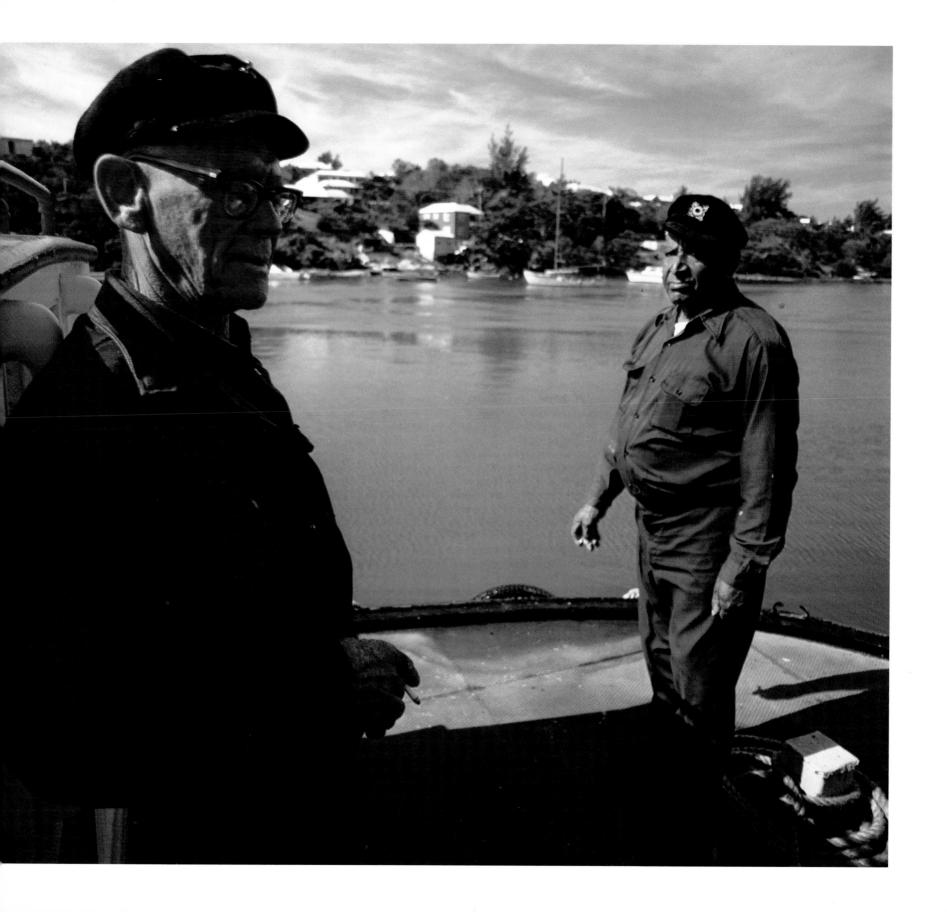

So, due to inclination and geography, Bermudians early turned to the sea for their prosperity—indeed, for their survival. It is a course which has influenced the island enormously throughout its history, for it has turned Bermuda toward the outside world and its developments, thus helping instill in its people, a receptive and modern outlook, to a degree rare in an island people.

On a more prosaic level, it meant that Bermuda

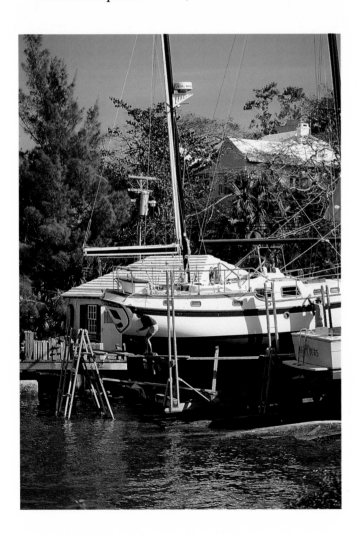

needed ships, and her shipwrights were soon fashioning the native cedar into some of the lightest, fastest ships afloat, the famed sloops, and later, in the 1800s, the even faster clippers. (Ironically, the advent of the steam age in the early 19th Century, which numbered the days of the wooden ship, also spurred shipbuilders to produce the fastest clippers ever, in an effort to remain competitive.)

The heyday of shipbuilding is long past, of course, but Bermudian boatyards remain on the scene (**this page**). Today, however, the work is largely maintenance and repair, and the vessels, rather than the legendary clippers, are likely to be sleek racing sailboats, pleasurecraft, or working fishing boats.

Another reminder of the days when the island's prosperity depended on its working seamen lives on in Bermuda's famed fitted dinghies, descendants of working sailboats which once plied her waters. Probably no form of sailing engages Bermudians' attention and sense of history more than the dinghy races held in late spring and summer. Dinghy racers are a dedicated and tiny group (only five active dinghies still exist), but the results of their bi-weekly races (including the season opener held annually in May in St. George's Harbour, **opposite**) are followed closely by a wide audience.

I talked with Norman Roberts, Mayor of St. George, who skippered his *Venture* (a dinghy which he had, as a boy, helped his father build) to a victorious 1979 season: "These boats are strictly racing creatures—probably no boat in the world carries as much sail for its size. In dinghy racing it's often not a matter of where you place—it's whether you reach the finish line at all!" Indeed, the boats have so little freeboard that every race day I witnessed during the 1980 season included at least one sinking. In a tight race, it is common to see one or more crew members leap off the stern—giving the dinghy a push forward which may put it first across the finish line!

Little remains of Bermuda's one-time involvement with the sea trades, as Bermudians have turned "inland" for their fortunes; but one activity has gone on much as it has for centuries: Bermuda's working fishermen arise before dawn, go down to their boats, and make for their favorite fishing areas, often jealously guarded.

I joined Eugene Barnes and his son, Michael, on the *Born Free* one morning to fish the western reefs. "It may get a little windy, so we'll leave the nets and haul pots today," Mr. Barnes said, referring to the wire-mesh traps built in such a way that a fish can enter but not exit.

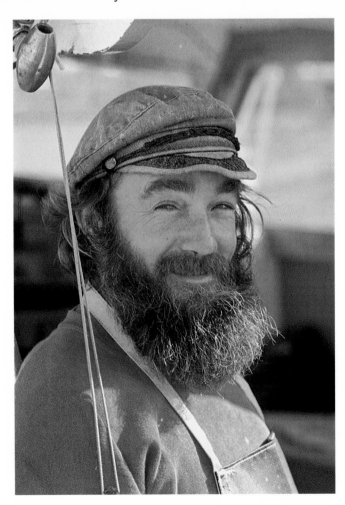

We had soon crossed the Great Sound from the *Born Free's* mooring near Point Shares and passed under Watford Bridge to the extensive reefs to the west of Somerset Island. In a sea-scape without apparent markings, Mr. Barnes steered a steady course, then slowed the boat, stood, and studied the sea ahead. "There, Mike," he shouted, pointing to port. Michael threw a weighted rope into the water, pulled, and a plastic buoy broke the surface, an attached rope leading to the "pot" on the sea bed. Mr. Barnes hurried down from the bridge to help haul the 80-pound pot aboard. ("I wish I had a nickel for every time I've been up and down that ladder," he remarked ruefully later.)

The pattern was repeated over and over (**opposite**) as we roamed the reef, pulling in parrot fish, snapper, jacks, groupers, and once, one of Bermuda's highly-prized lobsters ("He goes back," said Michael, "out of season.") Before long I had asked the logical (landlubber's) question: "Wouldn't it be a lot easier to find the buoys if they were on the surface?"

"Hah!" came the response. "We still have plenty of 'pirates' here in Bermuda." And secondly, after marveling at Mr. Barnes' ability to find some forty-odd buoys without any surface reference whatever—for it was nearly impossible to see a buoy until nearly over it: "How do you know where they are?" To which came a reply requiring no words at all—just a finger pointing to the side of his head.

"Things have changed a lot since I started in this business," Mr. Barnes, who will soon leave the *Born Free* and the sea to Michael, told me. "Today we keep nearly everything we find in the pots—days gone by, you couldn't have given away half the fish we sell today for good money. Trouble is, you wonder if there'll be any fish left 20 years from now. They're getting harder and harder to find."

It's a hard life, but one Michael looks forward to: "Lots better than working in an office or a hotel—you're out in the air, you're your own boss, and on a good day I can make as much as I would in a week in an office job."

Like Michael, bearded Paul Lavigne (**this page**), whom I photographed as he sold the day's catch aboard *The Rich One* tied up along Front Street, prefers the rigours—and rewards—of the fisherman's life, and thus helps keep alive Bermuda's long tradition of turning to the sea.

While Bermudians have plied the sea's surface since the colony's founding, the "last frontier" of the sea, to borrow a term, has awaited 20th-Century technology to become available to a wide audience. And it is, ironically, from that last, long-hidden province that have come reminders of man's earliest contacts with Bermuda—brief, unhappy contacts which led 16th-Century Spaniards to dub it "Isle of the Devils."

Symbolic of the treachery threatened by Bermuda's encircling reefs, as hypnotising today as when it was cast four centuries ago, a circular gold ingot flashes its brilliance in the Treasure House of the Bermuda Maritime Museum (**this page**). On its face are seals indicating payment of the royal tax, the Roman numerals "XX" indicating, probably, the tally number, and the name stamp of the official assayer. The treasure's route to Bermuda was a circuitous one, but it almost certainly began high in the Andes, where Incas had mined it and then fashioned it into extraordinary works of art. The *conquistadores*, seeing in these masterpieces only symbols of a pagan and inferior culture, melted them into ingots such as this one for easy transport to Spain.

The treasure fleets which carried bullion to Spain assembled each year at Havana, then took the usual route: northward on the Gulf Stream between Florida and the Bahamas, to catch the prevailing westerlies at about Latitude 32° N. The only obstacle in their path: Bermuda, with her extensive, deadly reefs. With the navigation and vessels of the day, many ships did not make it—among them, the *San Pedro* (wrecked in 1594, on the northern reef) and the *San Antonio* (1621, on the western).

Today a part of their treasure makes up the stunning collection of the Maritime Museum's Treasure House, housed at Dockyard. (The famed "Tucker Cross," found in the wreck of the *San Pedro* and reputedly the most valuable single object ever recovered from a Western Hemisphere wreck, was stolen from the collection sometime in the mid-1970s. Its whereabouts remain unknown.)

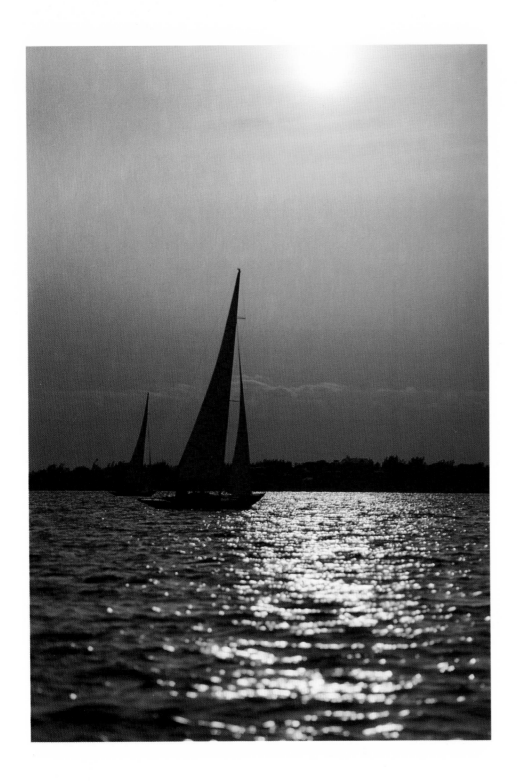

It is to Bermudian divers Harry Cox and Teddy Tucker that goes most of the credit for uncovering the spectacular treasures held by Bermuda's reefs; but even the amateur diver (as those seen, **previous page**, surfacing from a dive on the wreck of the *Mary Celestia*, a 19th-Century blockade runner) may find an old bottle or vase in one of Bermuda's scores of accessible wrecks, or simply discover that treasure awaiting any diver—the fantastic beauty of Bermuda's undersea world.

* * *

Considering the narrow confines of their increasingly-crowded island, it is hardly surprising that Bermudians continue to be irresistibly lured by the wide-open freedom and solitude of the sea. After all, where else can a Bermudian legally go more than 20 miles an hour—or find a bit of solitude to share with a sunset? (On **these pages** sailboats ply the waters of the Great Sound.)

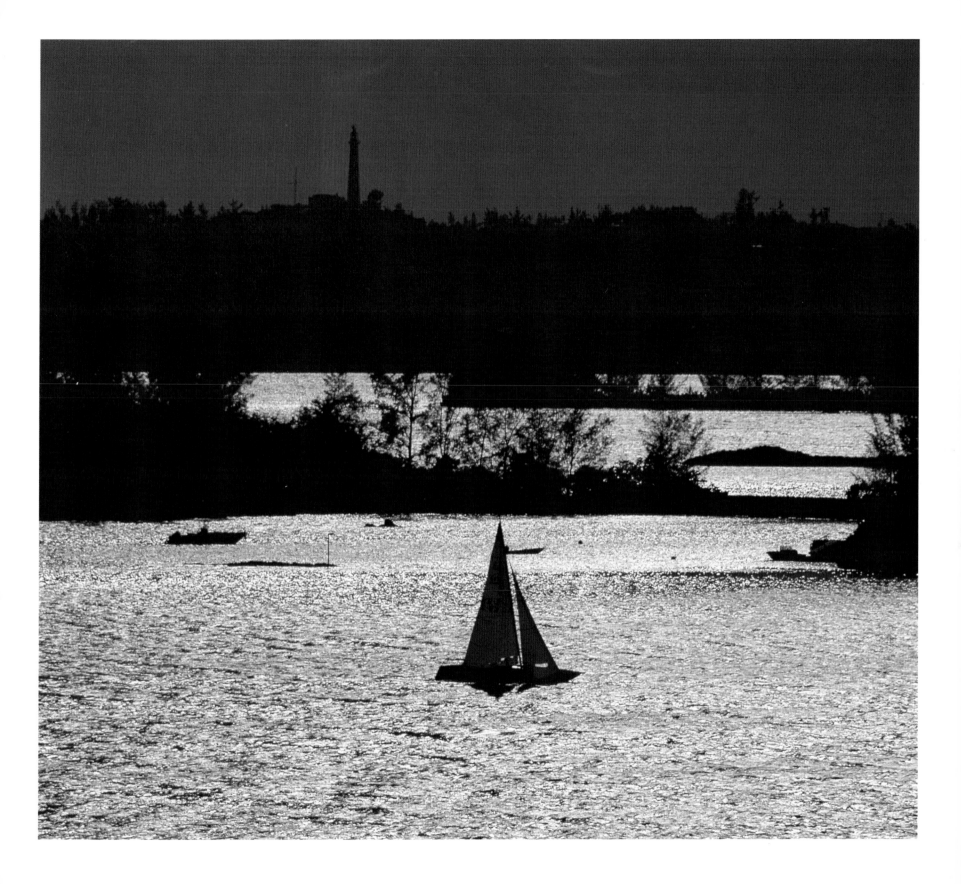

The Onion
Patch . . .

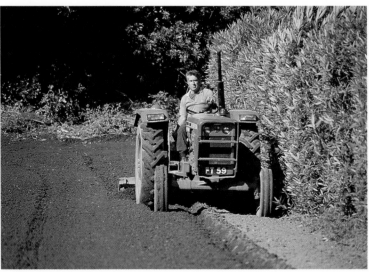

Considering how important has been the role of the sea in Bermuda's history, and Bermudians' traditional distaste for working the soil, it is ironic that in the latter 19th Century she gained a nickname reflecting the principal activity on the other side of her shoreline. Yet, the "Onion Patch" she became, as Bermuda onions (and potatoes, celery, carrots and tomatoes as well) became widely known and sought after in the northeastern United States.

As her historic economic mainstays connected with the sea began to decline in the mid-1800s, the vegetable trade grew to such scale that skilled farmworkers were in very short supply, especially after the emancipation of Bermuda's slaves in 1834 (for it was they who had performed the farm labor historically shunned by Bermudians). The solution was found in encouraging the immigration of Portuguese—already known for their agricultural skills—from the Azores. To this day farming, though no longer an export activity,* is dominated by Bermudians of Portuguese descent, although they have become prominent in commerce and the professions as well.

The many "fruit stands" dotting Hamilton and the parishes are, almost invariably, also owned and run by Bermudians of Portuguese origins, and the Tavares stand is no exception. Rain or shine, Maria Tavares (**this page, upper**) has dispensed her produce and good cheer for more years than she cares to remember, and has become a fixture on Middle Road in Warwick Parish.

Most of Bermuda's small plots are now worked by tractor (**this page, lower**), but one occasionally still sees the horse-drawn plough, especially when the soil is being worked to plant potatoes. Gerald Woolridge, shown (**opposite**), working "Major" in his potato field, is one of those few Bermudian farmers who is *not* of Portuguese ancestry. He came to the farmer's life in mid-career, after twenty-odd

*The flow of farm products has now been completely reversed, since the tiny area available for farming—little more than a square mile all told—is far short of needs. As with nearly all products consumed in Bermuda, the great bulk of foodstuffs are imported. It is, in fact, the duty on imports—about 30% in most cases—which provides the greatest portion of government revenues, since the island has no personal or corporate income tax.

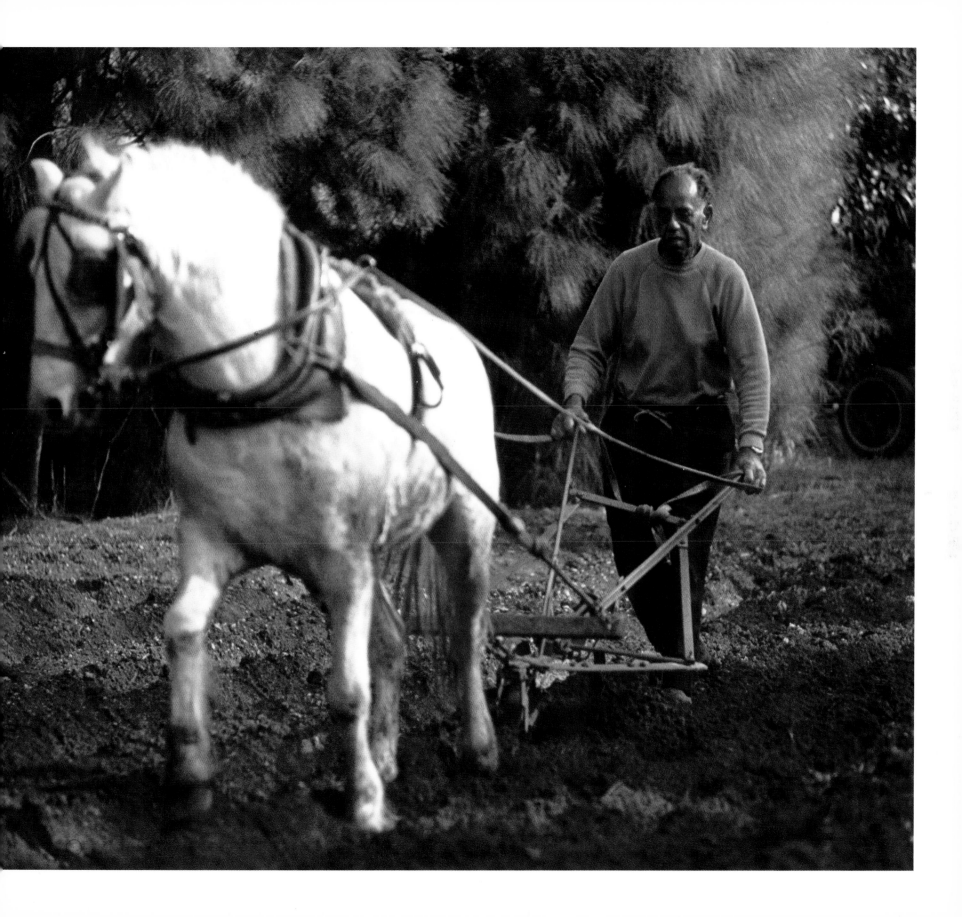

years in the restaurant trade. "I decided I was getting too old to put up with the foolishness you sometimes run into when people have had too much to drink," he told me. "This may pay a little less, but here's more to life than a few extra dollars." To residents of Warwick Parish he is afamiliar sight on Middle Road, driving his wagon to or from a field, his Scottie "Gigi" invariably at his side.

Farming vegetables for export came to an end in the 1930s, when the U.S. Congress enacted a protective tariff. But by then the seeds of the 20th-Century industry on which Bermuda's unprecedented modern prosperity is founded had been sown: for the very steamers which regularly carried Bermuda's produce to New York and Boston had, before the end of the 19th Century, begun carrying a few snow-weary Yankees to the sun and sea of Bermuda. The island's tourist industry was born.

It was perhaps not until that point that Bermudians began to appreciate that the lack of the natural resources on which a nation's prosperity is traditionally based (coal, mineral deposits, and water power, for example) was, in Bermuda's case, among her principal assets, for their absence meant that Bermuda had never undergone the industrial development which almost certainly would have spoiled her as a tourist attraction.

The Bermuda those early tourists encountered was in many ways markedly different from today's: naturally there were no motor vehicles (nor were there any anywhere else in the late 1800s); the pace of life was slower; the island was far less crowded (the population at the turn of the century was less than a third of today's); life was, for most, essentially a rural one.

And yet, the vital elements of the "Bermuda experience" which draws the visitor today were already present: the hospitality of the people, the quiet beauty of the island (**opposite**, a view of the Paget shoreline facing Hamilton Harbour) and the charm of the simple, unpretentious architecture Bermudians had fashioned in their island, visible in as prosaic a structure as a rustic gate near Spanish Point (**this page**).

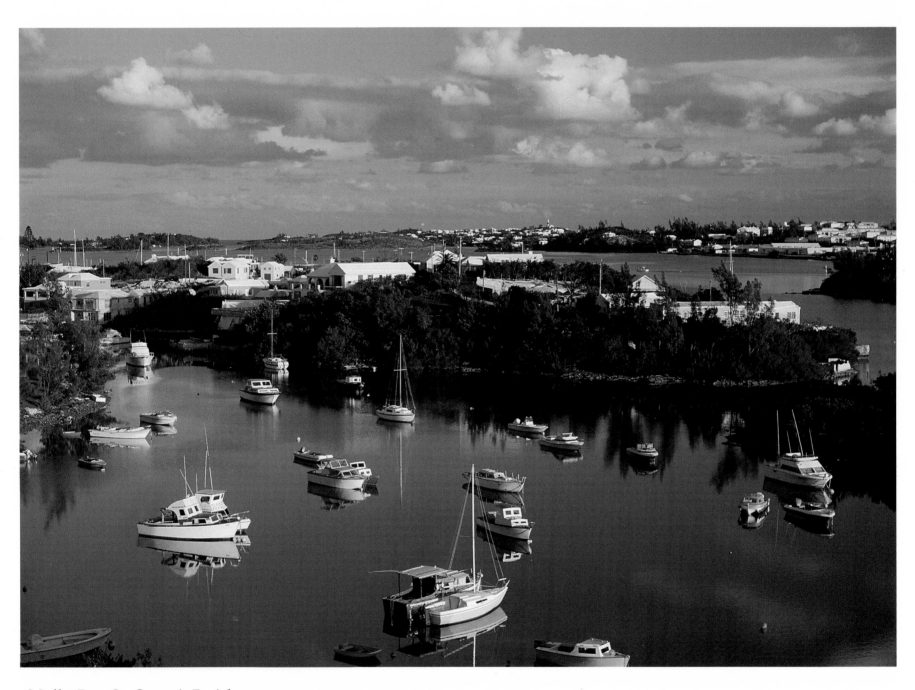

Mullet Bay, St. George's Parish

Looking east from Gibb's Hill (aerial)

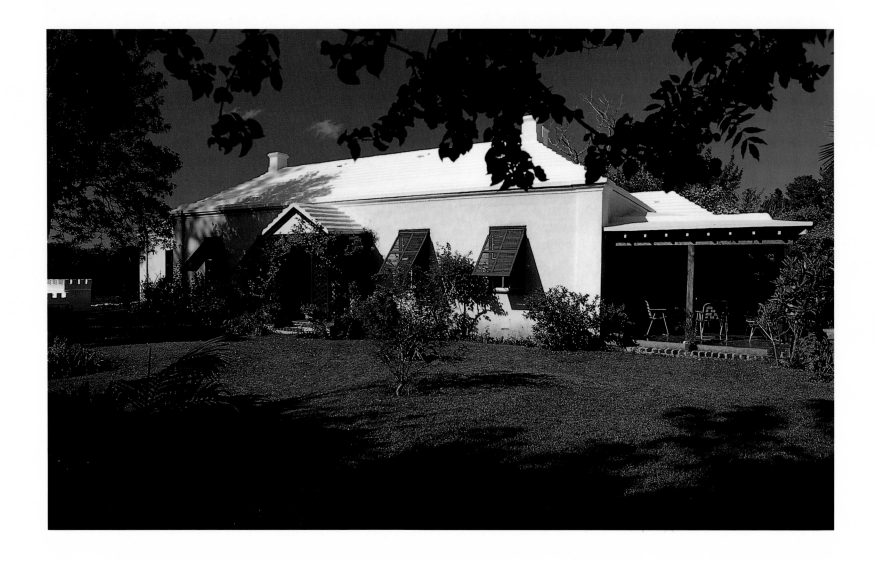

The adaptation of building styles to local conditions and materials (about which more on the following pages) resulted in the evolution of the classic Bermuda cottage, such as Stamp House (**opposite**), on the South Shore Road in Warwick Parish, and Shrewsbury, off Middle Road in Sandys Parish (**this page**). Shrewsbury has been in the same family since it was built in 1832 by the great-great-grandfather of the present owners, and takes its name from the ancestral birthplace in England. Stamp House, which dates from about 1705, is among the oldest cottages in Bermuda still used as a private residence; its name is recent, however, having come into fashion in the 1960s after the cottage served as the model for a Bermuda postage stamp.

As with all Bermuda homes, their white roofs double as catchments for rainwater, since the permeability of the islands' subsoil makes ordinary fresh-water wells an impossibility. Though the brick-red color of Stamp House is unusual in a land where pastels prevail, the walls of both houses—again, like those of virtually all Bermuda's limestone cottages—are plastered inside and out, to protect the soft stone from the erosion of rainwater.

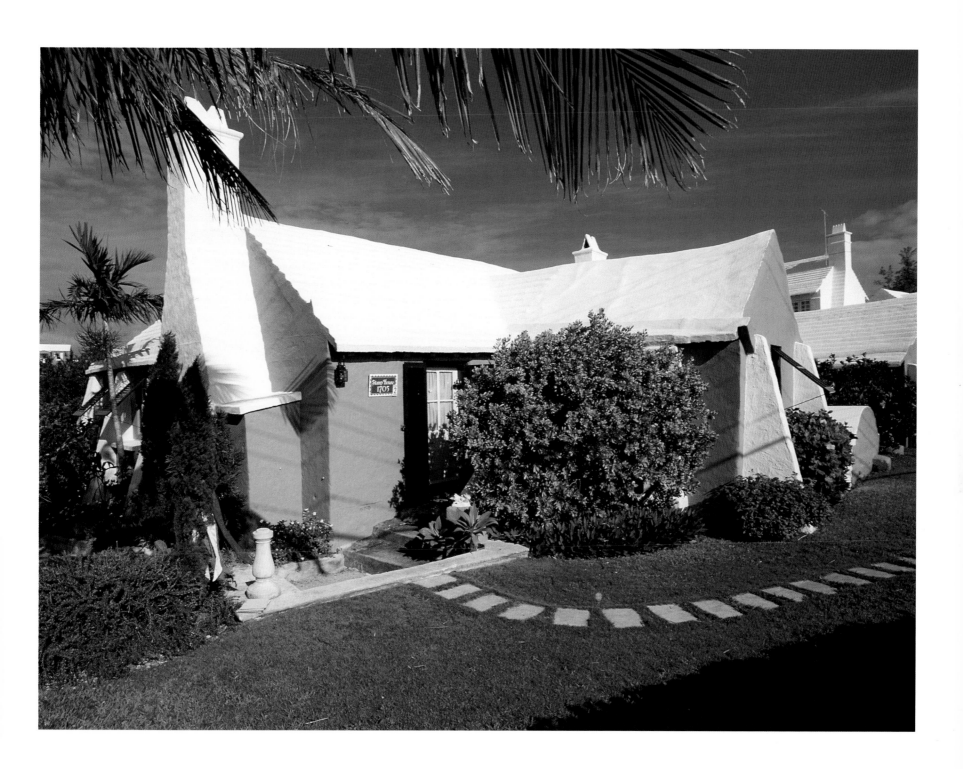

Indeed, many would argue that Bermuda's traditional architecture is its outstanding art form. As with all outstanding architecture, Bermuda's combined beauty with suitability to local materials and conditions: as with old European farm houses, nearly every feature of the Bermuda cottage has its logic, and the result are buildings which seem of a piece with the landscape.

The Bermuda builder began with two basic native materials: limestone and cedar. Seventeenth-century construction of cedar, wattle-and-daub, and palmetto thatch threatened to exhaust the cedar forests and proved too weak to withstand the hurricanes which periodically

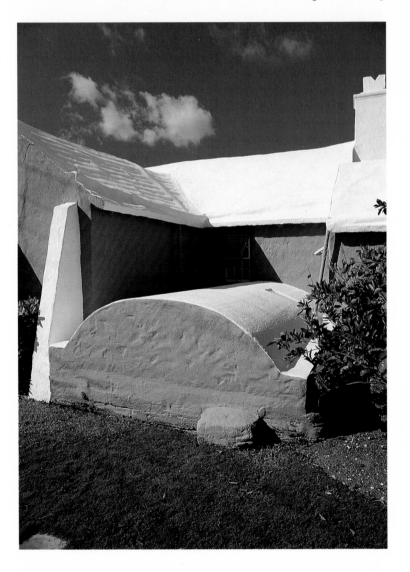

swept the island; thus from the 18th-Century onward, limestone was the prime building material for walls and roof, with cedar used for structural support, doors and windows, and for interior decorations.* The hurricane danger also demanded low, ground-hugging buildings with narrow eaves. The famous Bermuda "cake-icing" roof itself results from the overlapping of limestone slates, covered with a sealing mortar which is then painted or whitewashed; tapered or "stepped" chimneys economized building material while lending lateral support to the cottage **upper left, opposite page**).

Most building sites were sloped, owing to Bermuda's rolling topography, and Bermudians turned this feature to their advantage by carving a cellar into the hillside, resulting in an impressive two-story front while requiring the building of only one story in the rear (the excavation also provided stone for walls and roof); the tapered steps leading up to the front door were framed in what came to be called "welcoming arms," in reference to Bermuda's tradition of hospitality (**upper right, opposite**.)

Because the native limestone is so soft (it was historically quarried, and is still cut, with handsaws), and the climate so damp, it is unsuitable for fine exterior decoration; hence the simple, unadorned lines of the traditional cottage— a plainness which perhaps prompted the frustrated architect to indulge in an occasional, largely decorative "eyebrow" over a door or window (**lower right, opposite**).

A final touch in a larger home might have been a "buttery," a small outbuilding with thick walls and high, steep roof, which served to protect perishables against the heat. Even since the advent of refrigeration, many newer homes feature a storage building in the traditional buttery shape (**lower left, opposite**).

The rainwater captured on the roof of the house is channeled into a tank, or cistern. The advent of mechanized excavation equipment and the desire to conserve building space on smaller lots means that most modern houses have the cistern beneath the house itself, but with older houses the tank is commonly to the side, and at least partially above ground (**this page**).

*But each era has its dangers: after three-and-a-half centuries of cutting up the island for building material, Bermudians have come to realize that uncontrolled quarrying, too, presents risks to the island's beauty; today quarrying is carefully controlled, and concrete blocks and roof tiles of synthetic material often take the place of limestone in modern home construction.

Though the simple cottage sufficed for the average Bermudian household, as some Bermudian fortunes rose—especially as the sea trades came into their own with the 18th Century—so did the desire for grander houses. Perhaps most renowned of those larger houses is Mount Pleasant, high on a Paget hilltop overlooking Hamilton Harbour. As with many large Bermuda homes, it has been added to over the years (the wooden porches, seen in the frontal view, **opposite**, date from the 1860s, for example), a tribute to the quality of original construction—as well as to the thriftiness of those Bermudians!

A large collection of antique Bermuda and West Indies maps, dating from the 17th to the 19th Centuries, line the wall of the central stair hall (**this page, lower**), through which rises a splendid cedar staircase. The drawing room (**this page, upper**) ("You'll learn that the nicest room in these old houses was invariably called the drawivg room," Mrs. Elfrida Wardman, Mount Pleasant's owner, informed me with a laugh.) is a treasure-room of antiques, mahogany chairs from the late 18th Century, and a 19th-Century cedar cabinet.

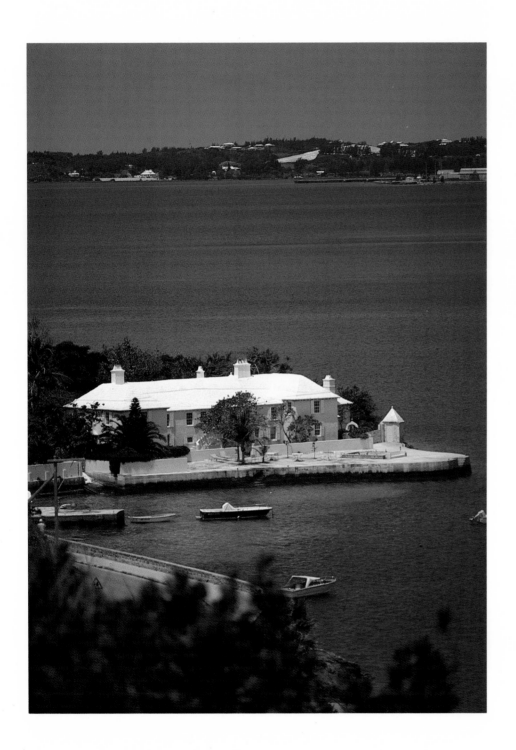

Some of the sea-faring home-builders preferred houses close to the water, where the structure could do double service as a residence and for commercial purposes. Thus Spithead (**this page**), built in the late 1700s on a point of land jutting into the Great Sound, served the famous privateer Hezekiah Frith as both home and warehouse. The story is told that Frith discovered the point of land on which Spithead sits to be a strategic location: a ship anchored on its western side was hidden from the view of anyone in Hamilton who might be looking—such as customs officials. (Much later, in the 20th Century, Spithead would have another famous owner: the American playwright Eugene O'Neill.)

No such ulterior motive has been attached to the location of Blackburn Place (**opposite**), just across Harbour Road from Darrell's Wharf on Hamilton Harbour—which suited admirably the needs of the 19th-Century sea captain Nathaniel Darrell (who used the ground floor as his warehouse and lived on the second story). Though part of the house dates from 1730, it, too, has been enlarged over the years, the front wings dating from 1820. The huge bay grape tree which shades the front lawn is said to be the largest, and perhaps the oldest, in Bermuda.

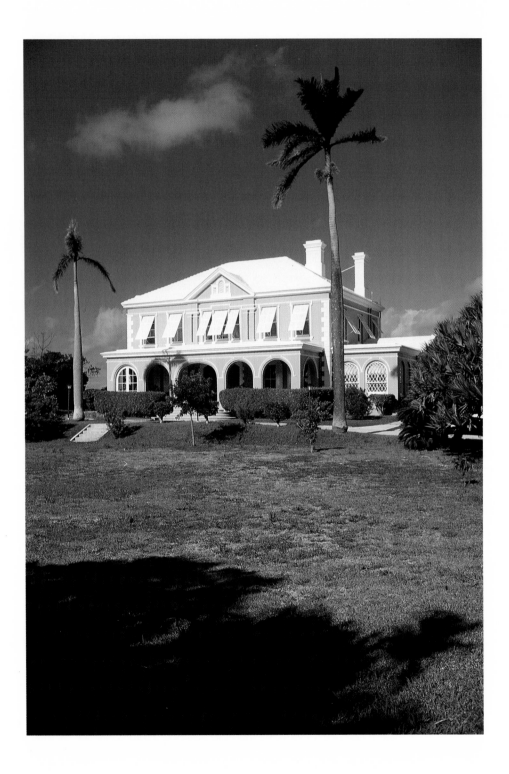

Bloomfield (**opposite**), another Paget Parish home overlooking Hamilton Harbour and the Great Sound, dates from the 1720s. Though grander in their aspect, most larger Bermuda homes nonetheless share many of the traits of the simple Bermuda cottage, from whose tradition they evolved. Thus they tend to complement, rather than clash with, the architectural landscape.

One characteristic common to early Bermuda homes, large or small, is the fact that it was difficult to find cedar logs which could yield beams longer than sixteen feet, which effectively limited the width of rooms, no matter how large the house. The solution in larger homes was often to build in an "E" or "U" pattern (as with Bloomfield) which yielded a larger structure without sacrificing flow-through ventilation.

As befits its name, Overlook (**this page**) also overlooks Hamilton Harbour from its location on Harbour Road in Paget. Like many of the houses built in more recent times, Overlook retains many of the architectural features of Bermuda's early classic houses and cottages.

And a characteristic of nearly all Bermuda homes, old and new, small or large, is the fact that they are *named*, rather than numbered. Many of the names, like those of Mount Pleasant, Bloomfield, Norwood, Somerset, and Rosemount, to name a few, evoke poetic or historic associations, while some others (I encountered "Wit's End," "Dream Come True," and "Just a Start," for example) reveal a more whimsical bent. Whatever their inspiration, the names of Bermuda's houses add to its storied charm. (And are sometimes the postman's headache!)

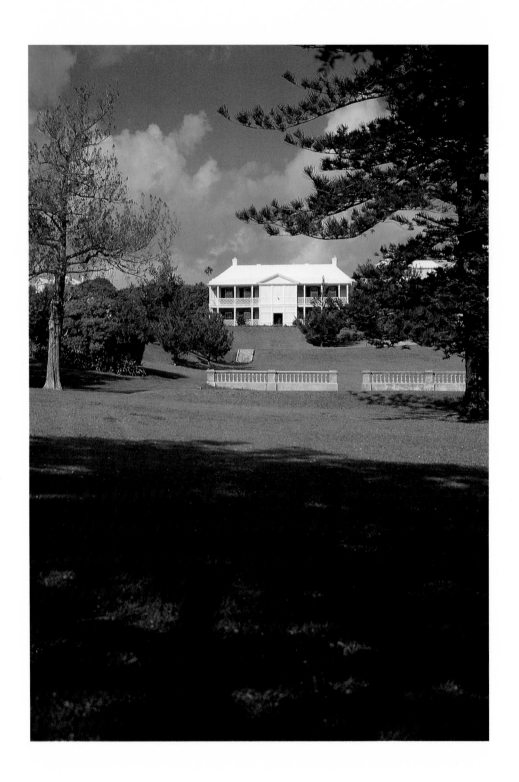

Camden, the stately centerpiece of the Botannical Gardens in Paget East, dates from the 1750s. Now the official residence of Bermuda's Premier, the house is the scene of official receptions and is open to visitors on a regular basis.

. . . and a
Few Onions

The appeal of Bermuda, it is often remarked, lies as much with the charm of her people as with her land. Whether it was a young schoolgirl (**this page**), whom I photographed hard at work in her school art class, or the mayor of Hamilton, I found a blend of openness, self-assurance, and a lack of pretense which made nearly every encounter a memorable one.

(Perhaps it is here, in fact, that I should remark that the time I spent "covering" Bermuda as a writer-photographer was one of the most pleasurable periods of my life. Having recently experienced another country

where a photographer was regarded with suspicion and often outright distaste, I was in a better position than most to appreciate the Bermudian traits I describe above. If this book seems overly laudatory of Bermuda, it is probably because it is hard to come away from the island with anything but a good feeling for the country.)

I first encountered Sir Henry Tucker in St. George as well, where he had agreed to pose for me in the historic Tucker House (**opposite**), where an earlier generation of the extended Tucker family had made its mark.* Perhaps no recent Bermudian has figured so prominently on the Bermudian scene as has Sir Henry. His public life has included thirty years in the legislature and service as Bermuda's first Government Leader under the 1968 Constitution (the equivalent of the Premier under today's terminology). His private life has been no less impressive: as head of Bermuda's largest bank, he, together with handful of others, was the moving force in Bermuda's becoming an international corporate, financial, and insurance center. Today the employment provided by over 4000 "exempt" companies (meaning enterprises incorporated in Bermuda, but doing business abroad) is second in importance only to the tourist industry, and constitutes a much-sought diversification of Bermuda's economy.

But the above is only part of his success—many have attained renown and material reward, and in the process gained the enmity of subordinates and the general public. Sir Henry, I discovered, is probably the most widely respected and liked man on the island—and, for me, nothing speaks so eloquently to that than the fact that this knight is known to one and all simply by his nickname, "Jack." ("I have no idea where that came from," he remarked with a laugh, "I got it as a boy, and it just stuck.")

*The Henry Tucker for whom the house is named was president of the Governor's Council when the colony was still in its formative years; he and his relatives figured prominently in the island's early history. Several later members of the Tucker family (including two Henry Tuckers of the 18th Century—obviously the family has had a fondness for the name) are portrayed on the walls beyond Sir Henry. The Tucker House is today a museum, filled with 18th-Century cedar antiques, and administered by the Bermuda National Trust.

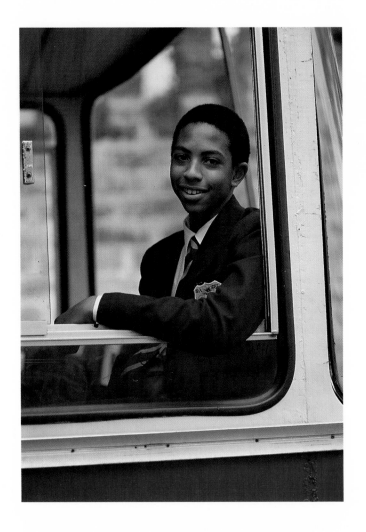

*Q*uo *Fata Ferunt* (Whither the Fates Lead Us) reads the country's motto. In 1979, the fates led a young woman from St. George, Gina Swainson, abroad to compete in the Miss World contest. Where the fates had led, her charm and beauty prevailed, bringing her the title and crown of Miss World. No Bermudian has ever struck a more popular response: her triumphant return to the island at the end of that year prompted a national holiday and parade through the streets of Hamilton, where thousands of Bermudians displayed their immense and genuine pride in their "home-town" girl's success. An equally enthusiastic welcome awaited her when she returned to lead the Bermuda Day Parade (**opposite**) in June of 1980.

Where the fates will lead Bermuda in the coming years is naturally a question of great import to her people. Much will depend on the employment opportunities the country manages to provide to the some 12,000 youngsters now of school age (like the young lad I photographed framed in a bus window at the Hamilton bus stand, **this page**) who will be joining the labor force over the next two decades.

Bermuda's combination of sky, water, verdant landscape, and pastel houses have long been an inspiration to the artist: the great American artist Winslow Homer visited Bermuda at the turn of the century and, stepping out of his usual medium of oils, produced a score of watercolors, including "Salt Kettle," painted in 1899 and now in the collection of the National Gallery of Art in Washington, D.C. (**this page, upper**).

In the ensuing decades many other artists, both native born and from abroad, have followed, including Alfred Birdsey (featured in the first edition of this book), whose abstract style of rendering Bermuda scenes has made him perhaps the best known of the artists now active on the Bermudian scene.

However, most of the watercolorists working today, such as Mary Powell and Carole Holding, prefer a more realistic style. A native of England who came to Bermuda to work in the hotel industry over two decades ago, Miss Holding (who is pictured on the **opposite page**) eventually returned to the passion for art she had felt in her childhood. The result has been the development of a charming "soft" watercolor style particularly suited to her two specialties: flowers and Bermuda scenes such as "Featherbed Alley, St. George's" where coincidentally she has her studio (**this page, lower**).

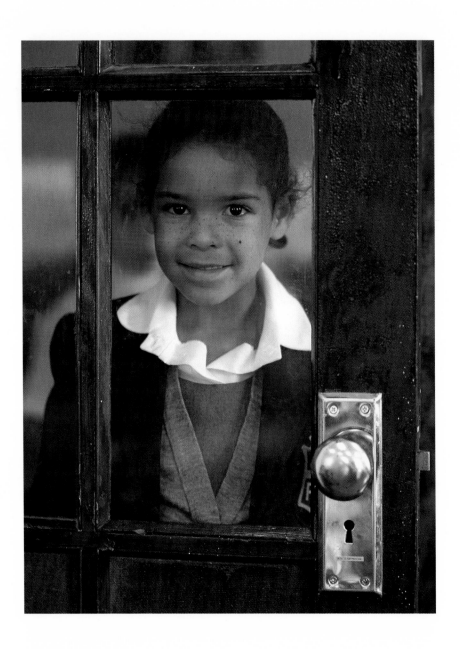

Sculptor Chesley Trott (**opposite**) has carved out a special place among Bermuda's artists by reviving Bermuda cedar as an art form; today his cedar sculptures—in both traditional and modern styles—command prices in the hundreds of dollars.

Throughout her early centuries, Bermuda cedar was the standard wood in the beams and trim of houses, and used by craftsmen for making both utilitarian and fine furniture—some antique samples of the latter now commanding prices in the thousands of dollars. Today, with the advent of economical mass production, these craftsmen have all but disappeared.

As a young man Mr. Trott—perhaps inspired by an aunt who was an amateur painter—saw in the cedar the possibility of developing a unique art form and the chance to restore to prominence cedar's role in Bermudian decoration. He was none too soon on the scene, for by that time suitable cedar logs were rapidly disappearing: as a result of the devastating blight which struck the cedar stands in the 1940s (see "Bermudiana"), the stricken trees were going up in smoke in Bermuda's fireplaces. Indeed, it is in no small part due to Trott's artistic success (and that of other sculptors, many of whom he has influenced as an art teacher) that Bermuda cedar has come to be recognized as a scarce national resource. Today the Bermudian homeowner carefully examines a log in his woodpile for artistic value before consigning it to the fireplace, and even the simplest handicrafts made of Bermuda cedar command a premium in Hamilton shops.

Framed in a cedar door at St. George's Preparatory School, a young first-grader gazes into the lens (**this page**).

Hamilton

The colony was nearly two centuries old before the city was even founded (in 1793), but Hamilton soon grew, due largely to its prime location, to be Bermuda's commercial and governmental center (the capital being transferred there from St. George in 1815). The capital's concentration of commercial buildings, and the fact that its tiny area (only 177 acres, compared with 341 for St. George) blends with heavily-populated Pembroke Parish which surrounds it, are deceiving, for it has a resident population of only 2000, making it one of the world's smallest capitals.

Though it is a modern urban center (albeit in miniature) and Bermuda's largest population concentration, Hamilton is ironically also where Bermuda's ties as a close-knit community are daily reaffirmed—for it is a rare Bermudian who walks down Reid Street without stopping two or three times to exchange a greeting or catch up on the latest news with a friend.

The widespread use of the motor vehicle since the 1940s has permitted the population to disperse throughout the island (Hamilton, in fact, has lost population over the past two decades, while that of the island as a whole has steadily increased), but Hamilton's importance today is no less than it was pre-automobile: a survey undertaken in 1972 revealed that most of the island's road traffic was bound to or from Hamilton, where resident and tourist are irresistibly drawn (during summer evenings, as **above**, the lights of cruise ships join with those of the city to make for a lyrical sight).

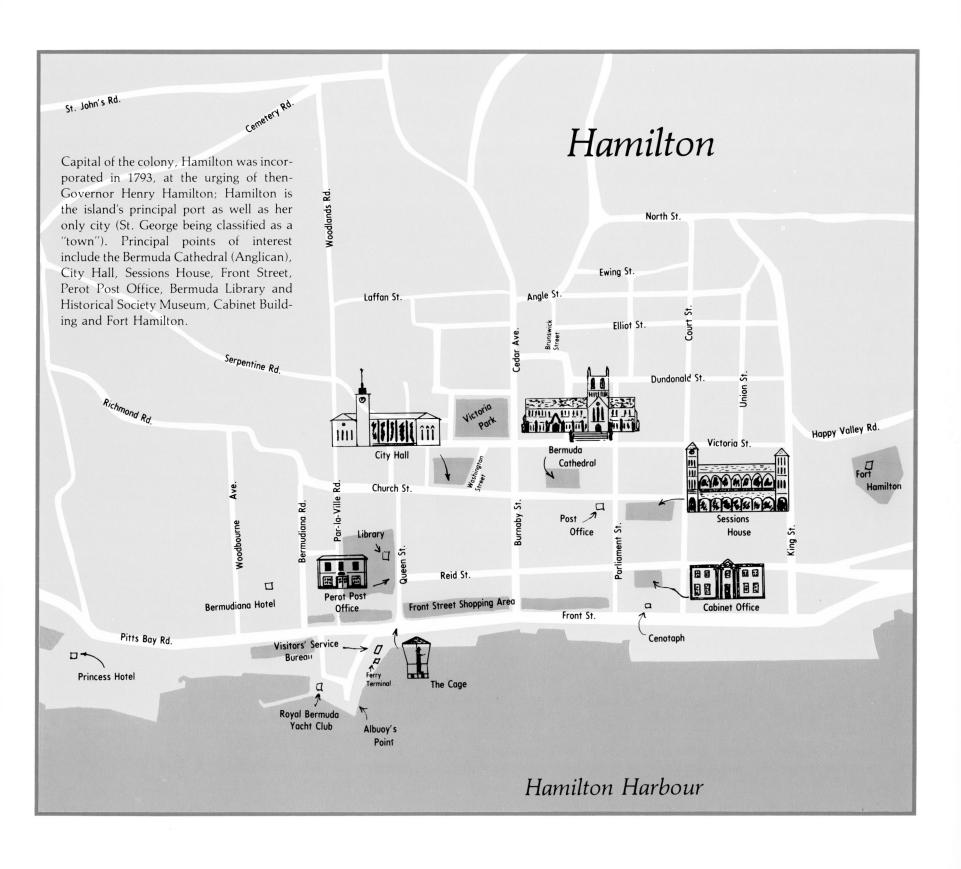

Hamilton

Capital of the colony, Hamilton was incorporated in 1793, at the urging of then-Governor Henry Hamilton; Hamilton is the island's principal port as well as her only city (St. George being classified as a "town"). Principal points of interest include the Bermuda Cathedral (Anglican), City Hall, Sessions House, Front Street, Perot Post Office, Bermuda Library and Historical Society Museum, Cabinet Building and Fort Hamilton.

St. John's Rd.

Cemetery Rd.

Woodlands Rd.

North St.

Ewing St.

Laffan St.

Angle St.

Brunswick Street

Cedar Ave.

Elliot St.

Court St.

Serpentine Rd.

Dundonald St.

Union St.

Richmond Rd.

Happy Valley Rd.

Victoria Park

Bermuda Cathedral

Victoria St.

Fort Hamilton

City Hall

Sessions House

Washington Street

Church St.

Woodbourne Ave.

Bermudiana Rd.

Par-la-Ville Rd.

Burnaby St.

Post Office

Parliament St.

King St.

Library

Queen St.

Reid St.

Bermudiana Hotel

Perot Post Office

Front Street Shopping Area

Front St.

Cabinet Office

Cenotaph

Pitts Bay Rd.

Visitors' Service Bureau

Princess Hotel

Ferry Terminal

The Cage

Royal Bermuda Yacht Club

Albuoy's Point

Hamilton Harbour

M ention Bermuda to the tourist who has been there, and very likely the first image that will come to his mind is Front Street (**opposite page**), where a panoply of storefronts representing the full range of the rainbow faces Hamilton Harbour (see **following pages**). It is here that Hamilton's leading shops, with labels known the world over, are located: shoppers browse through Scottish woolens, Irish linens, and English crystal, or perhaps consider purchasing a locally-made gold charm emblematic of Bermuda, such as a miniature longtail or fitted dinghy.

During the tourist season Front Street is aclamor with activity: an unending stream of taxis picking up their passengers, the shouts of carriage drivers directing their horses ("Come back!" you hear, as a driver backs his carriage into a parking space to await the next fare) and package-laden tourists crowding the arcade covered sidewalk.

On Church Street, a short walk up the hill from Front Street, the City Hall (**this page**) dedicated in 1960, incorporates elements of Bermuda cottage architecture into its design and is topped by the *Sea Venture* weathervane.

A Bermuda-blue sky sets off the Bermuda Cathedral (**opposite**), dating from the 1890s, and built in the Middle English style (a form of neo-Gothic). Seat of the Anglican Bishopric, the cathedral stands on the site of Trinity Church, destroyed by fire in 1884.

The Anglican Church of Bermuda dates from 1973, when its predecessor, the Church of England, was disestablished, perhaps in recognition of the developing trend toward local autonomy in Bermudian affairs. Although it retains the largest number of adherents, and through its predecessor, claims the longest history of Bermuda's Churches, the Anglican denomination today coexists with more than 25 others on the island.

I visited with the Cathedral's Canon, the Rev. Peter Hartley, one hot summer Sunday after services, as a throng of Bermuda-short-clad worshippers filed out of the Cathedral. "Looks like you're the only one at a disadvantage," I remarked, referring to his ankle-length surplice. "Not at all," he replied with a chuckle, "I've got my bathing suit on underneath this!"

Later, I visited the Canon's home, where members of the Cathedral's Ladies' Guild were busily turning out needle-point for the Cathedral's kneelers. Over the years the Guild has supplied over 300 of the kneelers for the Cathedral (like the ones pictured **this page**), each with an original design, many of them inspired by the scriptures.

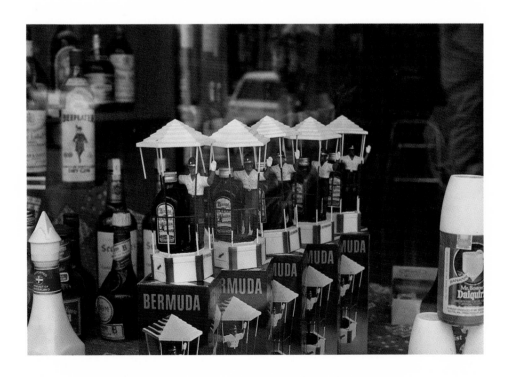

A youthful grin earns a greeting from a policeman on Reid Street (**opposite**). (Bermuda's policemen are not seen in their famous summer uniform until after May 24th, traditionally the first day on which Bermuda shorts are worn.) The island's police force follows the British custom of going unarmed; but Bermudians' preference for other types of work—especially in the high-paying tourist industry—means Bermuda must look abroad for a large proportion of its policemen, mainly to Britain and the West Indies.

Indeed, Bermuda's employment situation is an enviable one, since its major employment problem is a lack of skilled workers (such as nurses, accountants, and secretaries)—unemployment being essentially non-existent. The country fills its skilled needs by recruiting workers from abroad on a temporary permit basis.

Policemen at crosswalks and street corners are an increasingly rare sight, ever since Hamilton yielded to the fact of increased motor traffic and installed its first intersection traffic lights in 1978.

A miniature reproduction of Front Street's famed "policeman in the birdcage" serves a commercial purpose in a shop window (**this page**), where it promotes a locally-made liqueur.

A veritable wall of cruise ships disgorge eager tourists directly onto their new mo-peds ("The worst thing you can do is get behind someone who is worse on one of these things than you are," I overheard one chastened novice mo-peder advise her companion.), who jockey for position with wary veterans, including businessmen on their way to the office (**opposite**).

A pair of Bermudians, clad in that most famous of Bermudian inventions (**this page**), pause for a chat before Front Street's line of arcades. Perhaps no other facet of Bermuda's "personality" so surprises the visitor as the omnipresence of Bermuda shorts. ("Even the firemen wear Bermudas!" I heard one incredulous visitor say to another).

The visitor eventually grows accustomed to seeing businessmen on Front Street, policemen, and even the Anglican bishop, so attired, and, if he is sensible, he soon adopts the style for himself. (A personal note: Having lived in the Caribbean, where businessmen routinely wear suits—the long-trousered kind—through sweltering summers, I can only hope that other cultures will soon adopt this most intelligent of Bermudian habits.)

Pausing on Reid Street to share a last word with his passengers, a hire-carriage driver evokes a scene (**opposite**) reminiscent of a time before Bermuda knew the automobile, and horse-drawn transport was common. The Second World War saw the end of that era, when American military personnel, manning two island bases, utilized motorized transport. After the war the Bermuda legislature, perhaps not foreseeing the eventual consequences of the decision, narrowly approved the use of cars by the general public.

In spite of limits on automobile size and ownership (only residents are permitted to drive cars, and they are limited to one car per household), the arrival of the car—and later, the ubiquitous motorized cycle—inevitably altered the island's atmosphere (in both senses of the word). Many Bermudians continue to lament the presence of the noisy, smelly beasts (at least those belonging to others), and scarcely a week passes without some criticism of motor vehicles being aired in the local press.

Despite the invasion of the horseless carriage, the real article survives, lending a grace to Front Street, where a morning glory graces a carriage lamp (**this page**).

* * *

Reid Street honors a notable 19th-Century Governor of Bermuda, William Reid, who, among other accomplishments, greatly encouraged the island's agriculture, pushed for the construction of Gibbs Hill Lighthouse, and founded Bermuda's first public library.

Hamilton takes on a special charm as evening falls over the city. The noise and congestion of daytime traffic all but disappear, for Hamilton "goes to bed early." Quiet streets and passageways, like boutique-lined Chancery Lane, linking Front and Reid Streets (**this page**) become especially delightful for the pedestrian, and the 19th-Century Sessions House (**opposite**) assumes a particular beauty against the fading sky.

Bermudiana

Perhaps the most charming of Bermuda's endemic plant species is Bermudiana, the national flower, which produces a blossom about one inch across for a few weeks during April-May.

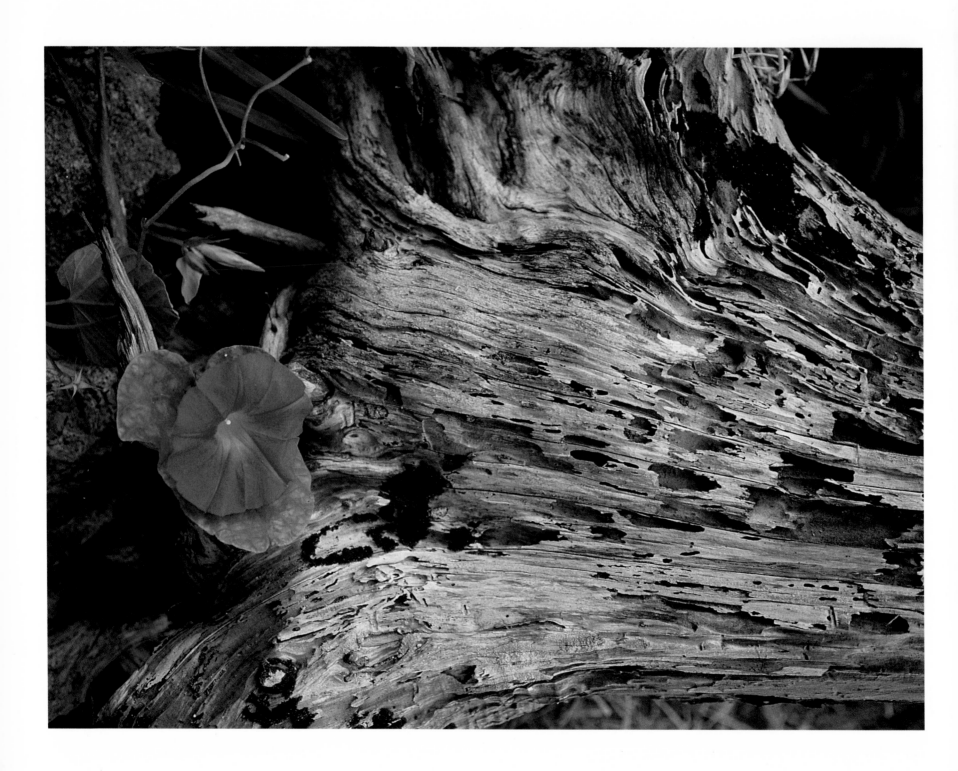

A strand of morning glory creeps across a fallen cedar stump lying beside Middle Road in Southampton Parish (**opposite**), a ravaged reminder of the role *Juniperus bermudiana* once played in the history of the island. Since the earliest days of the colony the cedars, which once covered the island, were vital to its development: in the roof beams of cottages, for furniture, and above all, in the construction of the boats and ships upon which Bermuda's economy depended. So important was the cedar that legislation prohibiting its export and requiring stone construction of houses had been promulgated by the advent of the 18th Century. But even legislation was powerless against the juniper scale, a blight which invaded the island about 1940, soon decimating the forests.

Reforestation with the fast-growing casuarina was begun in 1949, and the diseased, skeletal cedars were felled to make way. Today the scale-scarred stumps line the roadsides, often overlooked by tourists whizzing by on their mo-peds. Only a few scattered healthy cedars remain of that original forest, but a new enthusiasm for replanting the cedar gives some hope that the beloved tree may one day return to its former place on the Bermudian landscape.

The morning sun backlights a frond of a palmetto, another of Bermuda's endemic trees (**this page**). The palmetto played a vital role in the early years of the colony's existence, when it was used for thatching the roofs of the settlers' homes.

Although something over 150 plants have been identified as endemic or native to Bermuda, the vast preponderance of the vegetation seen today has been introduced by man. Among the most popular of the introductions are the many varieties of hibiscus (**opposite page**), and the spectacular bird of paradise (**this page**).

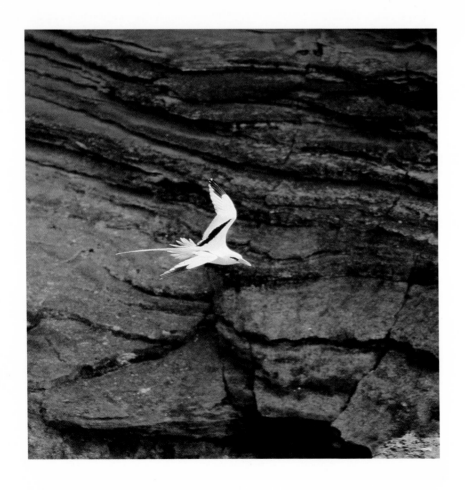

Much as was the case with the Hawaiian Islands in the Pacific, Bermuda's extreme isolation from continental land made it next to impossible for flightless land-dwelling animals to reach its shores alive. The only known native (that is, not introduced by man) land-dweller is the rock lizard, or skink, which is now very rare except on a few of the islands of Castle Harbour. (Two or three other lizard species, introduced by man, are more commonly seen.)

Another of man's introductions, the tiny whistling frogs from the West Indies, are very rarely seen, but hardly rare: and during the warmer months these tiny tree frogs (**opposite page**) insist on making their presence known, issuing their piercing calls into the night.

The islands were more accessible to birds, among them a local variety of petrel known as the cahow, whose great abundance made them a ready food source for Bermuda's earliest settlers, but which now face extinction; and the unofficial emblem of Bermuda, the migratory tropic bird, or longtail (**this page**), which nest in the coastal cliffs from spring to early autumn.

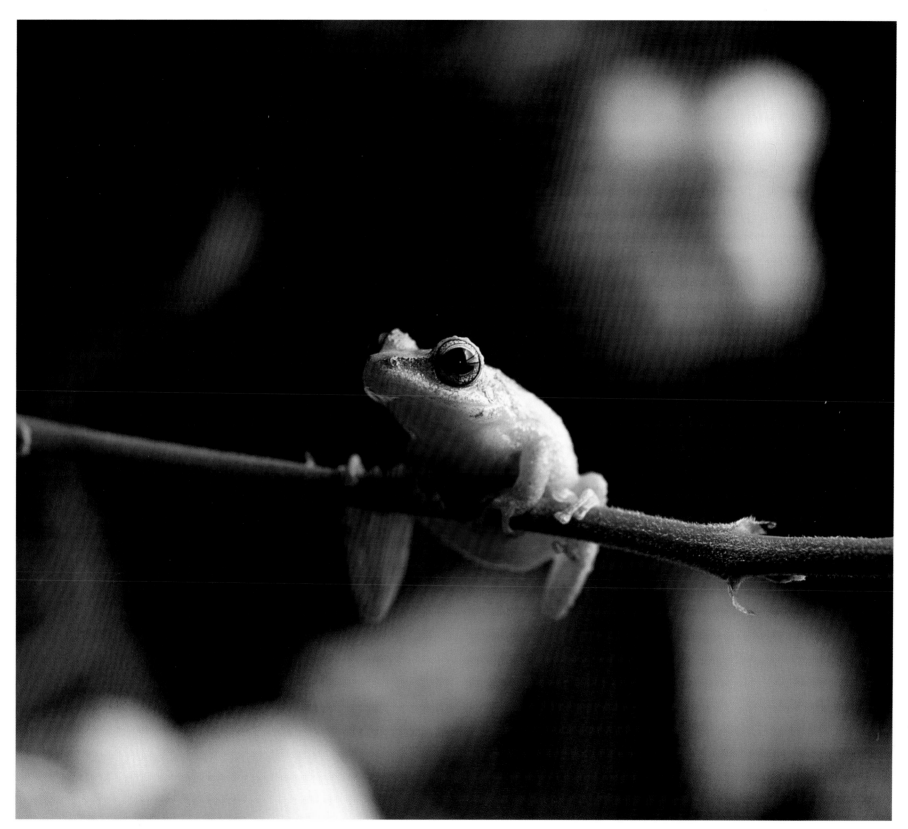

Actual size about one inch in length.

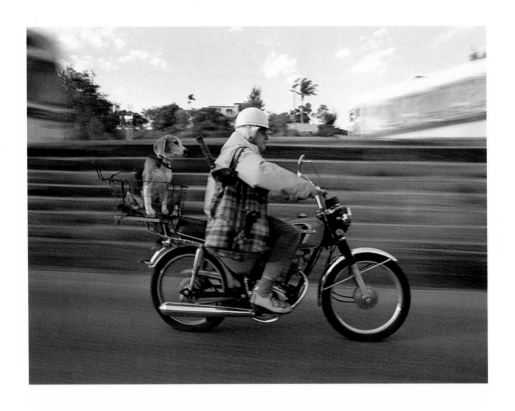

Contestant and owner stand inspection before the judge during an all-breeds show held annually in late spring (**opposite**). Several dog shows throughout the year draw entrants from the U.S., Canada, and Britain, as well as from Bermuda's own hundreds of dog fanciers.

Dog lovers are not the only competitors drawn to Bermuda's shores: bridge players flock to international tournaments, while golfers are attracted by events at the island's six 18-hole courses. But perhaps most renowned among Bermuda's competitions are her sailing events, such as the Newport-Bermuda Yacht Race, held in June of even-numbered years, when several thousand racers, friends and family—as well as those simply drawn to the festive atmosphere—descend on the island for the finish and the partying that follows.

A dog lover after his own fashion, architect Peter Leitner takes "Tacsko" along to a tennis game (**this page**).

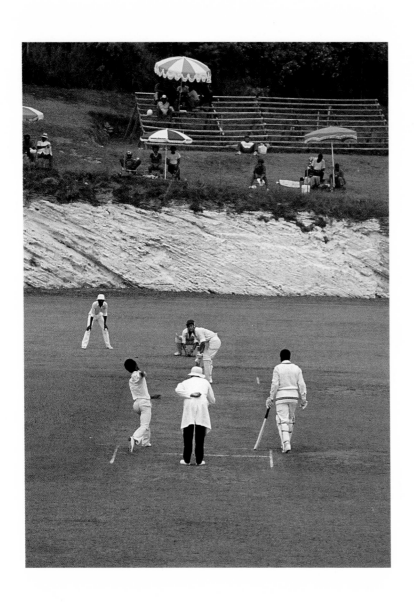

Traditional whites, decorum, an almost stately atmosphere—appropriate to a game emanating from Imperial Britain—characterize a cricket match in progress at Southampton Oval (**this page**). The season finishes up with Cup Match, that annual festivity (held in commemoration of Emancipation Day, August 1, 1834) when the entire island goes half-crazy over cricket.

But if cricket has tradition on its side, it is sometimes rough-and-tumble soccer which seems more in tune with modern tastes. Here (**opposite**) a Devonshire Rec team (in yellow) battles it out with Dandytown under a winter drizzle.

For many of Bermuda's visitors, as well as her residents, the sport of choice is golf, and the island boasts no fewer than eight eighteen-hole courses, including spectacular Port Royal in Southampton Parish (**opposite**)

Students at Warwick Academy (**this page**) sharpen their skills on the violin in a music class, part of a thorough academic and extra-curricular program offered by the school, which seeks to combine elements of both British and North American approaches to education. The Academy boasts an august scholastic tradition dating back to 1662—making it the oldest of Bermuda's schools, and one of the oldest in the Western Hemisphere.

A total of more than 40 institutions, both private and public, compose an educational system guaranteeing free, compulsory education through the secondary level, and have created one of the world's lowest illiteracy rates. A limited program of higher education is available at Bermuda College, but students seeking to attend university must go abroad (most choosing Britain or North America).

Learning their trade from the kitchen floor up, a class of hotel administrators-to-be at Bermuda College's Department of Hotel Technology learn meal preparation in the school's restaurant kitchen (**this page**).

"As dependent as we are on tourism," the department's head, Martin Barnes, told me, "we can't afford anything but first-class people in our tourist industry. So we teach future administrative personnel how to cook as well as how to manage—how else can they properly supervise a hotel kitchen?" But above all, he continued, "We try to instill an attitude of excellence, a pride in service. It's vital to this business, and once lost, almost impossible to regain. We plan never to lose it."

(A meal in the school's restaurant later revealed excellent work in the kitchen and eager, if not yet fully polished, attention by the students in the dining room.)

Small wonder that Bermuda tends carefully to her tourist industry: as an island essentially without raw materials or manufacturing, tourism directly accounts for close to 40% of her total employment, and for an even greater share of her prosperity. Thus Bermudians have a very big stake in maintaining the elements that have made their island a "quality tourist destination," to quote the guidebooks.

This is not to suggest that Bermuda is a paradise where no problems exist: the same moped, for example, that is generally seen as a quaint means of transport takes on a different aspect when a "pack" of youthful riders tear around a blind curve with scant regard for the center dividing line. And even Bermuda's roadsides, spanking clean compared to most, are beginning to accumulate the trash of a "throwaway" society. Other problems, involving employment opportunities, educational quality, and housing, to name a few, impinge as well.

But such problems, at least at their present level, are serious only within the Bermudian context: the island is, on the whole, so beautiful and well-run, its population on the whole so prosperous, that any deviation from the ideal tends to assume a magnified import.

Given the pride Bermudians hold in their island, and their concern that it remain one of the truly idyllic places in the world for resident and visitor alike, it is more than probable that visitors will be coming to share a bit of the Bermudians' special world for generations to come.

Three off-duty sailors from a visiting Royal Navy ship find a touch of home in one of Bermuda's pubs as they sample a bit of that famed Bermudian hospitality (**this page**).

Wherever you roam in Bermuda, the roads are bordered by limestone—either a solid wall, where a "cut" has been made through a hill, or by drystone or "slave" walls (named after their original builders), composed solely of rough-cut limestone blocks carefully fitted together. Being Bermuda, they are usually graced with the lush vegetation, such as morning glory or nasturtium—or perhaps a mere common thistle—which leads to comparisons with Eden (**this page**).

And being Bermuda, a way was found to give even a prosaic wall a bit of enchantment. Though often disclaimed as a part of the "true" Bermudian architectural heritage, the moongate (**opposite**) nonetheless speaks of a part of Bermuda's past, when her sloops and sailors roamed the globe, bringing home from the Far East oriental vases which to this day decorate grand Bermudian homes, and bringing home as well an idea for decorating Bermuda's walls. Despite the disclaimer, the moongate has become a romantic part and parcel of Bermuda's landscape.

Bermuda
Revisited

A decade has passed since my first visit to Bermuda to begin the photography for the first edition of this book. In the ensuing years I have been fortunate enough to return to those enchanted isles several times, and though each visit has been very short, compared to the six months of my original visit, on each occasion I have taken my cameras, hoping to elaborate on my initial photographic impressions.

I discovered that this was not an easy task: Bermuda is a small place, and my initial coverage had been exhaustive in terms of my creative ideas; with each new visit, I tended to see the islands as I had originally recorded them a decade ago. Still, over the past decade I have evolved as a photographer, and some of the new photographs in this revised edition (scattered throughout the book as well as in this chapter) reflect that evolution. As I commented in that first edition, I believe Bermuda's traditional cottage architecture is her outstanding art form, and several of the new photographs emphasize that tradition.

In addition to the new subject matter, I have rephotographed a number of subjects which for various—usually technical—reasons I was never quite satisfied with in the first edition. (To take one example: I had never been entirely happy with the night photograph of St. Peter's Church in "Beginnings," for I had originally intended this to be a twilight shot. However, on the evening I had arranged for the church to be open, a passing rain shower delayed the shoot until the sky was entirely black. Through the courtesy of Brian Craddock, the rector of St. Peter's, I was able to arrange a new photo session, and this time the heavens cooperated.) It is astonishing to note, however, that even in a place as seemingly changeless as Bermuda, how frequently it is impossible to recreate a photograph: trees grow larger, or new buildings are erected which intrude on the photographic vantage point (true with the Bermuda Cathedral). Conversely, the trees of the Old Naval Cemetery on Ireland Island (seen in "Endings") were uprooted, broken, and stripped of their branches by Hurricane Emily in 1987, making that photograph impossible to duplicate, at least for the near future.

As for the people and the "feel" of the island, these are of course aspects much harder, especially for the outsider, to assess in a short visit, and I cannot presume to speak from the perspective of one who has known Bermuda from the "real" early days, before the automobile, mass tourism, the jet plane, and the widespread prosperity which is today taken for granted. As I noted in the first edition, paradisiacal as she sometimes appears, even Bermuda is not impervious to the problems which afflict the "outside" world to a much greater degree. I remember attending a cocktail party during my first visit at which it seemed that the principal problem facing Bermuda was the "wild dog" problem. Today, with drugs, crime, and racial questions increasingly in the news, the days when the island's main problem seemed (to some at least) to be scavenging wild dogs must be a fond and distant memory indeed.

That said, for me Bermuda remains as enchanting as I found her ten years ago, the place among those I have covered to which I most eagerly look forward to returning. In my own case, Bermuda's special appeal lies in her unique ability to combine the blessings of the modern world with "small town" friendliness and civility. I hope and trust that when the time comes to revise this book again, these words will be as true as they are today.

Tucker's Town (aerial)

Harrington Sound

Building facade, Burnaby Street

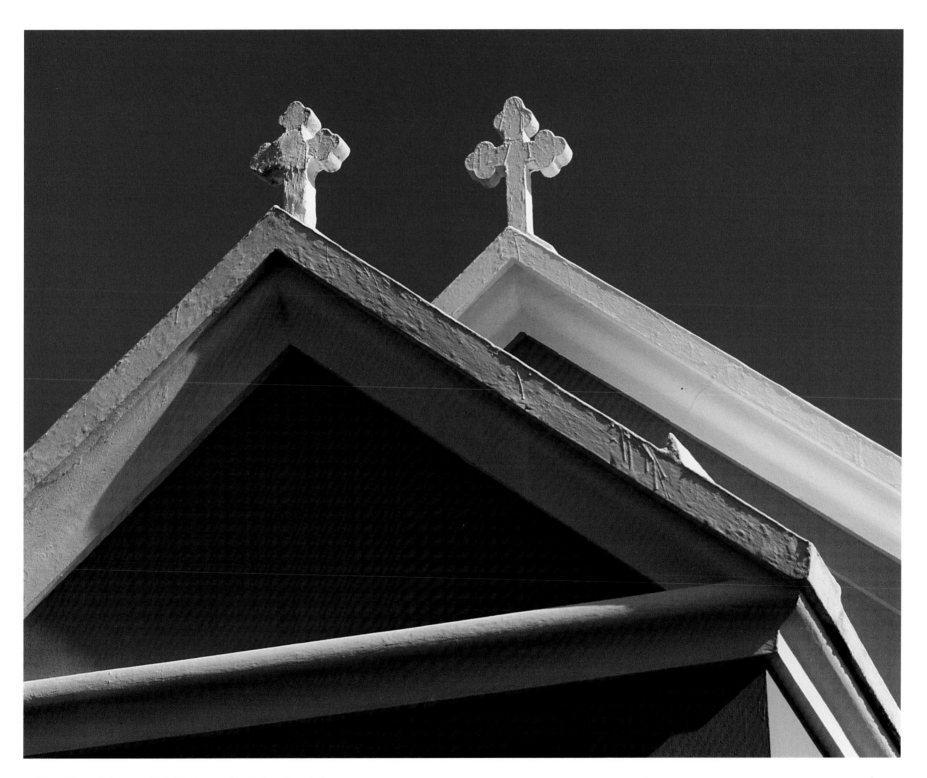

Roofline, Minstrels' Gallery, Smith's Parish

Roofline, St. George

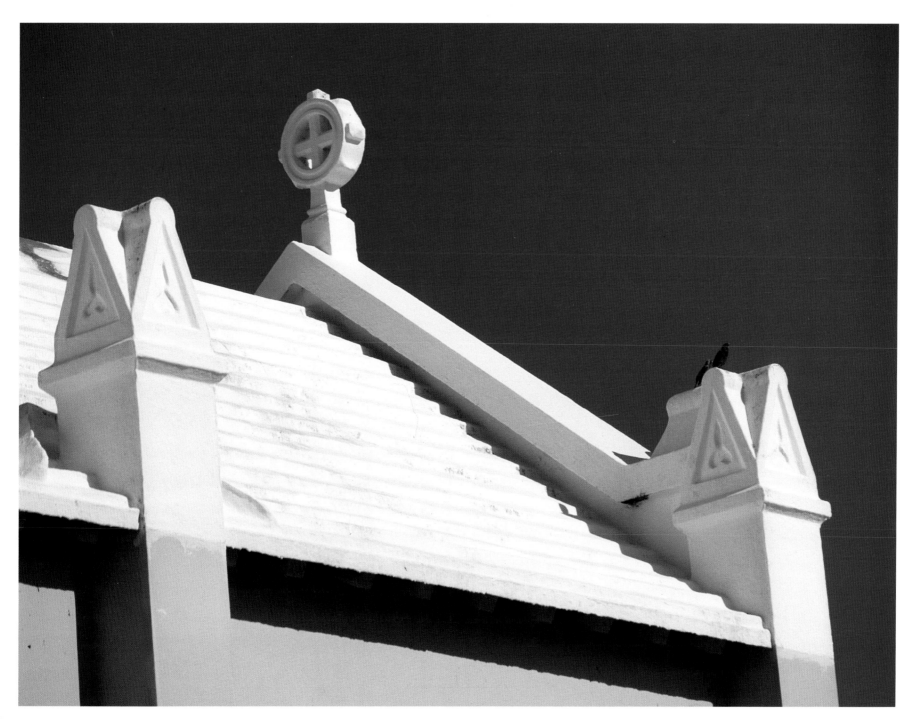

Roofline, St. Paul's Church, Paget Parish

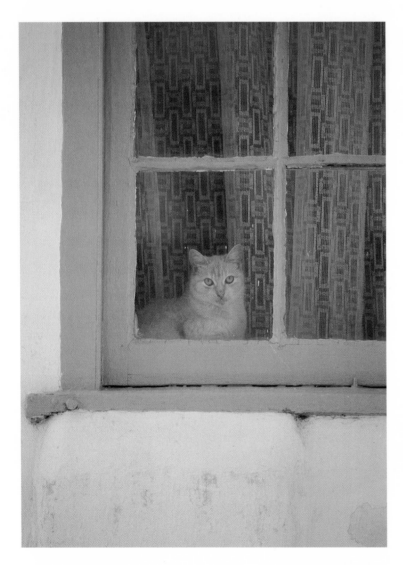

Window, Duke of Kent Street, St. George

Blockade Alley, St. George

Some of the flowers that make Bermuda a garden paradise: the plumeria, or frangipani, (**this page**), and four varieties of orchids (**opposite**).

Endings

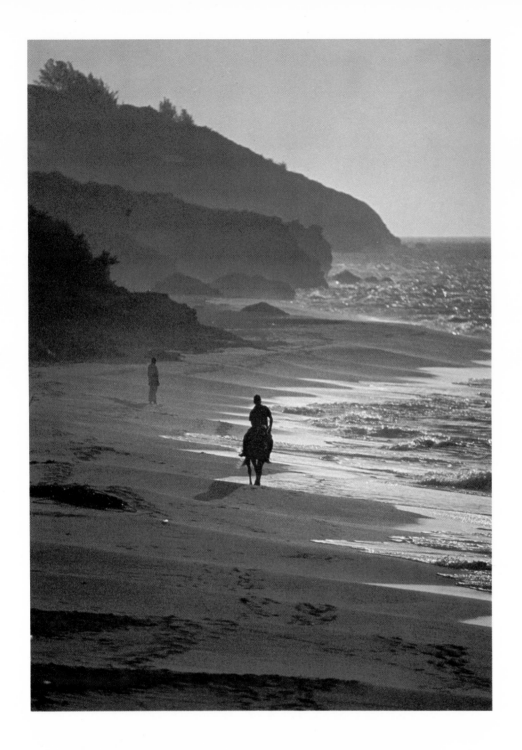

Two scenes from Bermuda's timeless symphony of light, land, and water: on **this page** an early-rising equestrian shares the solitude of Warwick Long Bay with a lone beach stroller on a summer morning; and a late-afternoon ferry departs the Salt Kettle landing (**opposite**) as the sun sinks into the clouds beyond Somerset.

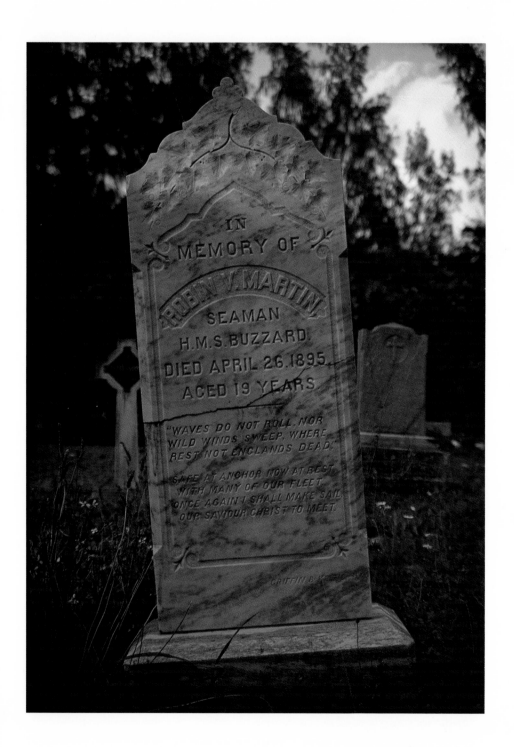

In a small glade beside the road on Ireland Island, just before the traveller reaches the Dockyard, is the old Naval Cemetery. It's worth a visit, a short walk among the headstones dating from the past two centuries, reminders of the era when Britain was a great sea power, and of Bermuda's role in that era. The headstones recall young men, mostly, . . . victims of explosions, disease, drowning . . . headstones of sailors who came to rest far from home. (The inscriptions describe accidents of station, rather than battle deaths, for throughout its nearly four centuries of settlement Bermuda has been—apart from scattered pirate attacks in the 17th and 18th Centuries—free of the ravages of invasion and warfare.)

As I walked in the cemetery late one afternoon, reflecting on this part of Bermuda's history, I chanced upon the headstone pictured here, and was greatly moved by the poetry of its inscription—an inscription which spoke the quiet dignity and pride of an earlier era:

Waves do not roll, nor wild winds sweep,
where rest not England's dead

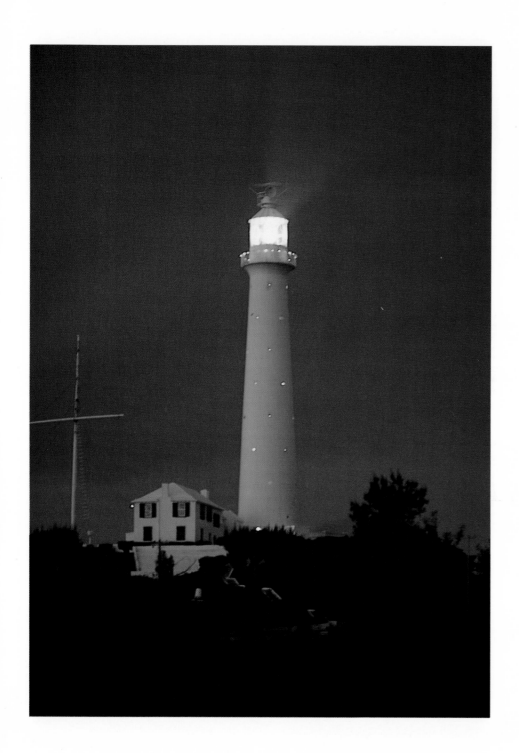

A beacon familiar to mariners and tourists alike, Gibb's Hill Lighthouse (**this page**) has crowned Gibb's Hill in Southampton Parish since 1846. The tower was erected after years of wrecks and a series of pleas from then-Governor William Reid; one of the first lighthouses ever constructed of cast-iron, the structure was brought in sections from England.

Still, its half-million candle power beam has not removed all the hazards of navigating Bermuda's waters: ships continue to go aground on the island's reefs (one as recently as late 1978, when the freighter *Mari Boeing* grounded on the northern reef).

Hamilton Harbour sleeps in the pre-dawn light of a summer morning (**opposite**).

Significant Dates

1503-09: generally-accepted period for Bermuda's discovery by the Spaniard Juan Bermúdez (the exact date is uncertain, but it had certainly occurred by 1515).

1515-1609: numerous sailors, mostly Spanish or Portuguese, sight, land on, or are wrecked on Bermuda, thus becoming the first people known to have set foot on the island; 1543 is the date on "Spanish Rock," believed to have been inscribed by one of these Spanish or Portuguese seamen. During this period the Spanish consider establishing a colony on the island, but fail to do so.

1609: the *Sea Venture*, part of an English fleet bound for Virginia, is wrecked on Bermuda's reef on July 28; after spending ten months there, all but two of the survivors continue on to Virginia. Since Bermuda has been continuously inhabited since this date, it is considered to mark the beginning of Bermuda as a settled place.

1612: having received glowing accounts of Bermuda's commercial potential, the Virginia Company of London receives a charter from King James I to colonize Bermuda as well, and sends out 60 settlers to found a colony. The Town of St. George is founded.

1615-22: Richard Norwood surveys the island, dividing the land into shares, and completes the first detailed map of Bermuda, from which nearly all early maps are derived.

1620: first meeting of the colony's Assembly held in St. George; this marks the beginning of representative government, the earliest in the British Commonwealth outside the British Isles.

1684: the Colony's charter is forfeited by the Bermuda Company (successor to the Virginia Company), and the Colony comes directly under the Crown's administration, although Bermudians retain the right of limited self-government.

1793: City of Hamilton founded.

1810: construction begins on Ireland Island on the Royal Navy Dockyard, which becomes a major naval installation and source of employment for Bermuda until its decommissioning in the 1950s.

1815: transfer of the seat of government from St. George to Hamilton.

1834: emancipation of Bermuda's slaves on August 1.

1861-65: during the American Civil War, Bermuda serves as a base for Confederate blockade runners.

1941: leasing of land for and commencement of construction of American bases in Southampton Parish and on St. David's Island.

1946: introduction of motor vehicles for general use.

1968: April—rioting, primarily racial in origin, occurs after Floral Parade, opening a decade of scattered civil disturbances and strikes. June—first written Constitution comes into effect.

1970: celebration of 350th Anniversary of Bermuda's Parliament.

Acknowledgments

From the experience of having been a reader far longer than a writer, I know that this is a section often overlooked or given short shrift by most readers. It should not be so, at least not with a book of this nature, for it owes a great deal to the cooperation of an untold number of people. Working in Bermuda, as I have mentioned elsewhere, was a great pleasure for me as a photographer, for Bermudians were—nearly unanimously—splendidly helpful in providing access (balconies, rooftops, etc.) and delightfully willing as subjects.

The contribution of many people will be apparent from the text or from the credits at the photographs themselves, but sometimes considerable efforts were expended for material which was eventually not included, and I would be remiss if I failed to say a special "thank you" to:

Doug Wheeler, as able and willing an assistant as a photographer could ask for; Doug, Andy Miller and Kathy Brem, for their generous hospitality; Charles Webbe of the Bermuda News Bureau, for countless favors and guidance; Sydney Corbett and Gary Phillips, Bermuda Post Office; Mrs. Elizabeth Storey, Anson Nash, and the staff of the Bermuda Maritime Museum; U.S. Navy (U.S. Naval Air Station, Bermuda); Bermuda National Trust; Mayor Norman Roberts and crew of "Venture"; Harry Powell and crew of "Vixen"; Capt. Jan Konig and crew of "Oleander"; "Stumpy" Mello; "Wink" and Hal Kempe; Devon Curtis; Mr. & Mrs. Ford Baxter; George Trott, Crown & Anchor Restaurant; Warren Hallamore; Emily Fox; Bob Lee; Foxy Cooper; George Rushe; Angelino Madeiros; Armando Moniz; David Wingate; Antoinette Butz; Mr. & Mrs. Thomas Wall; Alma "Champ" Hunt; and to Martha Hoch and Marie LaBrucherie, for their assistance in the editorial process.

Notes

It will be clear to the reader that *Images of Bermuda* is not an in-depth study of Bermuda's past or present. For the reader wishing a fuller treatment, I would recommend both Terry Tucker's *Bermuda, Today and Yesterday*, and the splendid work of William E.S. Zuill, Sr., *Bermuda Journey: a leisurely guidebook*. Additionally, *Bermuda: As a Matter of Fact!* provides an excellent quick-reference guide to facts and figures of historical and current significance.

* * *

The photographs for *Images of Bermuda* were shot on Kodachrome and Agfachrome films, with Nikon cameras and various Nikkor lenses, ranging from 15mm to 500mm in focal length. For underwater photography I used an Ikelite housing affixed with a dome port.

Though I feel there are a number of excellent camera systems, for the last 10 years I have used Nikon equipment, for one principal reason: I believe they are unmatched in reliability and ruggedness. One brief incident may suffice to demonstrate that: I had parked my mo-ped in a driveway off Harbour Road one evening to get some shots of a ferry, putting a camera in the cycle basket for a moment while I set up my tripod. I heard a crash, turned, and saw that the cycle had fallen against the stone wall, throwing the camera over the wall and down a steep embankment, where it came to rest on a sidewalk. Fearing the worst, I hurried down to inspect the damage—only to find my fears unfounded: there were only some scratches, a small dent, and plenty of dirt to be cleaned off. Body, meter, and lens still functioned perfectly.

Exposure information is not given because it is simply too inconvenient to note it down in most of my shooting. Besides, in most cases the direct through-the-lens meter reading was used; in difficult lighting situations I recommend plenty of bracketed exposures. The current edition of *Images of Bermuda* is the distillation of over 8000 photographs.

Bermuda
(or Somers Islands)

Location and geography: island group composed of more than 120 islands with a total land area of approximately 21 square miles (53 sq. kilometers), located in the western North Atlantic Ocean (32° 18′ N., 64° 45′ W.) about 570 nautical miles (1046 kilometres) east of Cape Hatteras, North Carolina, the nearest point of continental land. Bermuda is the exposed tip of an extinct volcano, capped by a layer of aeolian limestone of a generally hilly aspect (maximum elevation, at Town Hill, Smith's Parish: about 260 feet, or 79 meters).

Population: 57,000 (1990 est.); nearly all the population is located on the seven principal islands joined by bridges (the population has approximately doubled since 1940); population density among world's highest.

Government: British colony, internally self-governing under a written constitution. Crown-appointed Governor responsible for foreign affairs and security matters. Parliament (oldest of British Commonwealth countries outside British Isles, dates from 1620) elected by universal adult suffrage.

Economy: based principally on tourism; "exempt" companies (foreign-operating, locally registered) are second-largest employment source. Per capita income one of ten highest in the world.

Climate: mild, humid, sub-tropical, moderated by Gulf Stream; rainfall distributed fairly evenly throughout year; daytime temperature in "warm" months (April-November) in mid-70's and 80's F. (20's C.); in "cool" months (December-March), 65-70 F. (low 20's C.).

Motto: *Qua Fata Ferunt* (whither the fates lead us).

Author-photographer with a few friends: Roger LaBrucherie is a native of El Centro, California. Educated as a lawyer and economist at Harvard College and Stanford University, Mr. LaBrucherie served in the U.S. Peace Corps in the Dominican Republic in the early 70s, an experience which he credits for developing his interest in investigating and interpreting far-off places.

In addition to the present volume, he has published books on the Dominican Republic, Barbados, Puerto Rico, and Hawaii.

Grouped around him are students of Mrs. Powell's Nursery School, Friswell's Hill, Devonshire.

Design consultant: HOCHdesigns, Los Angeles

The Homer print on page 80 is courtesy of the Henschel Collection, National Gallery of Art.

Images of Bermuda (Revised Edition)
Copyright 1992   Roger A. LaBrucherie

Imágenes Press
P.O. Box 1080
Pine Valley, California 91962
Tel: 619-473-8676/Fax: 619-473-8272

Printed in Hong Kong
10 9 8 7 6 5 4 3

ISBN 0-939302-21-7 (Trade edition)
ISBN 0-939302-22-5 (Deluxe edition)